OUT OF A DISTANT LAND

To Margaret,

Jill + I have enjoyed getting to know you while in Spartanburg. Your sweet smile + kindness have been a real blessing. May you continue to be blessed as you continue being a blessing — In love,

Gary
11/07

OUT OF A DISTANT LAND

Testimony, Parables, and Devotions of a Prodigal Son

GARY BOND

Pleasant Word
A Division of WINEPRESS PUBLISHING

© 2003 by Gary Bond. All rights reserved.

Printed in the United States of America

Packaged by WinePress Publishing, PO Box 428, Enumclaw, WA 98022. The views expressed or implied in this work do not necessarily reflect those of WinePress Publishing. Ultimate design, content, and editorial accuracy of this work are the responsibilities of the author.

No part of this publication may be reproduced, stored in a retrieval system, or transmitted in any way by any means—electronic, mechanical, photocopy, recording, or otherwise—without the prior permission of the copyright holder, except as provided by USA copyright law.

Unless otherwise noted, all Scriptures are taken from the New Inernational Version of the Holy Bible.

Verses marked NKJV are taken from the *New King James Version*. Copyright © 1979, 1980, 1982 by Thomas Nelson, Inc. Used by permission. All Rights Reserved.

ISBN 1-57921-551-3
Library of Congress Catalog Card Number: 2002116752

To Jill, my life's partner, whose love never failed

Because those who are led by the Spirit of God are sons of God. For you did not receive a spirit that makes you a slave again to fear, but you received the Spirit of sonship. And by him we cry, "*Abba*, Father."

Romans 8:14–15

Contents

Preface 11

Part One - Testimony 13
1. Out Of A Distant Land 15

Part Two - Used By God 27
2. My Favorite Hammer 29
3. A Christmas To Remember 32
4. Bite Off More Than You Can Chew 39

Part Three - Share The Good News 43
5. Free Indeed 45
6. The Perfect Gift 49

Part Four - Growth—A Daily Choice 53
7. Like A Tree 55
8. Light Post To Light Post 59
9. The Full Moon 65

Part Five - Live It Now 69
   10. What Would It Look Like 71
   11. Tuit 75

Part Six - Hard To Be Humble 79
   12. How We Forget 81
   13. I Am The Man 85

Part Seven - Buzzwords 91
   14. Rights 93
   15. Moderation 99

Part Eight - At His Feet 105
   16. Worth It 107
   17. The Five Senses 111
   18. Junk Drawer 117

Part Nine - In His Steps 123
   19. Run The Race 125
   20. A Mirror's Beauty 129
   21. Defining Moment 133
   22. They Opened Their Eyes 139

Part Ten - Gone Fishing 145
   23. The Big One(s) That Got Away 147
   24. Not Just A Fly Rod 161
   25. The Always Pool 167

Part Eleven - His Amazing Ways 171
   26. God Works 173
   27. God Doesn't Add 181
   28. One More Time, Daddy 187
   29. I Wish I Was God 191

30. The Tar Baby 195

Part Twelve - His Amazing Grace 201
　31. Lee 203
　32. The Final Inning 209
　33. 2000 213

Part Thirteen - True Riches 217
　34. Who Wants To Be A Millionaire 219
　35. Drop The Bag 223
　36. Lifestyles 229
　37. I Need 235
　38. Is It In You 239

Part Fourteen - When The
Going Gets Tough 245
　39. By Design 247
　40. Springer Mountain 251
　41. Endurance 257

Part Fifteen - Knowing Him 265
　42. Do You Want To Breathe 267
　43. Biography 273
　44. The Whisper Of The Heart 279

Part Sixteen - What's Left 283
　45. All The Ingredients 285
　46. I Was Here 289

Part Seventeen - Relationships 295
　47. Related By Blood 297
　48. Father's Day 301
　49. Mother's Day 305

50. Charlie 309
51. Partners 315
52. Sonship 321

Epilogue 329

PREFACE

This book begins with the story of a wayward son. It ends with the story of sonship. Between are the devotions to a Father and to a Son.

My life changed in September of 1991. How God has revealed himself and worked in my life since enables me to share these devotionals. Most were given during the period that I served in adult Sunday school at Prince Avenue Baptist Church in Athens, Georgia.

So much of my early Christian life was spent in the shallows. Since my roots were also shallow, I was uprooted by the winds of temptations that came my way. My prayer is that this book will aid Christians who find themselves in the shallows and long for a deeper, more personal walk with our Lord.

The purpose for writing this book is actually three-fold:

(1) That Christians will gain a deeper insight into God's truth by observing him speaking in ordinary, everyday experiences.
(2) That Christians who find themselves lost in a "distant land" will "come to their senses" and return to a waiting, loving Father.
(3) That his Word of truth will touch someone lost in the slavery of sin and that they will be led to the freedom and salvation of Jesus Christ.

Each devotional is designed for your active response. Please read with that in mind. Let the Lord speak to you through his Spirit, and then apply his truth to your life. Keeping a notebook of your responses will also be helpful.

Although I cannot write as one who is fully mature, when I consider how God has worked in my life over the last decade, I have the hope that I will know the fullness of his purpose and that I will finish strong. Only through the incomprehensible, amazing grace of God am I able to share these moments in my walk with the Lord. Join me in that walk.

Part One

Testimony

CHAPTER 1

OUT OF A DISTANT LAND

Jesus told this parable:

"A man had two sons. The younger son told his father, 'I want my share of your estate now, instead of waiting until you die.' So his father agreed to divide his wealth between his sons.

"A few days later this younger son packed all his belongings and took a trip to a distant land, and there he wasted all his money on wild living. About the time his money ran out, a great famine swept over the land, and he began to starve. He persuaded a local farmer to hire him to feed his pigs. The boy became so hungry that even the pods he was feeding the pigs looked good to him. But no one gave him anything.

"When he finally came to his senses, he said to himself, 'At home even the hired men have food enough to spare, and here I am, dying of hunger! I will go home to my father and say, "Father, I have sinned against both heaven and you,

and I am no longer worthy of being called your son. Please take me on as a hired man.'"

"So he returned home to his father. And while he was still a long distance away, his father saw him coming. Filled with love and compassion, he ran to his son, embraced him, and kissed him. His son said to him, 'Father, I have sinned against both heaven and you, and I am no longer worthy of being called your son.'

"But his father said to the servants, 'Quick! Bring the finest robe in the house and put it on him. Get a ring for his finger, and sandals for his feet. And kill the calf we have been fattening in the pen. We must celebrate with a feast, for this son of mine was dead and has now returned to life. He was lost, but now he is found.' So the party began.
Luke 15:11–24 (NLT)

It was late summer of 1971. I was 18 years old at the time, so I knew everything. But I headed off to college just to make it official. The college I had chosen was Berry College, just outside of Rome, Georgia. Attending Berry had been a dream of mine for the last two years of high school, and the much-anticipated day to begin had finally arrived.

Driving through the front entrance that day, I remember seeing the words written on the low brick wall, "Gate of Opportunity". Indeed, many opportunities already had been provided, and many prayers had been answered. Scholarships and grants were awarded that enabled me to attend without financial hardship. What great plans and dreams I had as I passed through that gate!

Testimony

The opportunities that awaited me resulted from what I believed to be God's plan for my life. When I was eight years old I became a Christian, and I was raised in a Christian home. During the summer before my senior year of high school I had answered a calling into the ministry. A commitment was made before my church to follow that calling.

Offers to preach in area churches followed immediately after that announcement, and in November of 1970 my home church licensed me into the ministry. During that licensing service I recall standing before the congregation and stating in all confidence, "God has called me to preach, and nothing in all the world can stop me!"

Before the end of the first quarter at Berry College, however, I made a choice that was to affect the next 20 years of my life. That choice was having my first drink of alcohol. If asked now the biggest regret of my life, I would say without hesitation that it was the taking of that first drink. Practically all other regrets stem from that one choice.

Guilt was the feeling I remember the morning after my first drinking episode. But not long afterward I had another evening of drinking, and giving in to the temptation became easier and easier. Soon I began to rationalize my actions by saying, "I may be going into the ministry, but I have a right to have fun and enjoy these college days. I am human, and, after all, it's not like I'm going to be an alcoholic."

Slowly, however, I became addicted to the escape, the lie, and the deception of alcohol. Drinking became increasingly frequent, and during my sophomore year it became an almost daily habit. Yet, I still managed to hide my addiction from many. The Berry College Chapter of the Baptist Student Union even selected me as president. But the consequences of alcohol were taking their inevitable toll. By the end of that sophomore year at Berry College, I had lost the will to go on, because I was totally out of God's will. I quit going to classes. My days were centered on the next drink and the other sin that it brought along. There was a total lack of discipline and self-control. Those words I had said with such confidence only a couple of years previously—"Nothing in all the world can stop me!"—seemed empty now. Something in the world had stopped me.

My grades the last quarter of the second year were all F's. Indeed, I had failed and failed miserably. I had brought shame to my family and myself. And, above all, I had shamed the name of Christ.

In May of 1973 I dropped out of Berry College and left behind a trail of broken dreams and broken relationships. From that moment I decided to live for myself and for my own desires. Just as the prodigal son of old, I took all I had and headed off into a distant land.

The next three years were spent jumping from job to job and never finding my niche. During that time the alcohol never stopped flowing, and I became increasingly dependent on its daily escape from my failures. Yet, during this period I met a girl named Jill, and we became friends.

Testimony

In autumn of 1977 I decided to join the Air Force. Perhaps, I reasoned, this would give me a chance to finish college, to collect my thoughts, to find my purpose, and maybe to rid myself of the chains of alcohol.

Following basic training and avionics school, I was assigned to Myrtle Beach AFB. Myrtle Beach, South Carolina was not exactly a great place to "sober up". The bars, clubs, beach parties, and drinking buddies were plentiful. Rarely did I pass up any opportunities for the wild beach life. The package store on the Air Force base offered cheap booze, as well, and was only closed on Christmas Day. They knew me there as a regular patron.

Sin and self gripped my life. My conscience was only a distant memory, because I was in a distant land.

In May of 1981 I was almost killed in an electrical accident while working on a piece of avionics equipment. Ten thousand volts of electricity coursed through my body. Only a miraculous circumstance saved me and kept the electrical charge from going through my heart.

During my three-day stay in the hospital following the accident, an airman from my squadron came to visit. Airman Pimble walked into the room carrying a Bible under his arm. He began to talk to me about the way that God had spared my life. He told me that God had a plan for my life. (How dare he tell me of God's plan for my life! That was all in the past and was only a distant memory.) My response was telling him that I only wanted to be out of the hospital and back out on the beach. It was the longest period I had been without a drink in years, and I missed that above anything else.

As I sent Airman Pimble on his way, I will never forget the look of disappointment on his face as he walked out the door. He had tried to reach me after my brush with death, but I couldn't be reached. I was still in a distant land.

At the end of 1981 I was discharged from the Air Force. Some things had been accomplished despite my waywardness. My college degree was complete. I had developed a relationship with that friend named Jill, and we were soon married. She did not know the chains of alcohol that had me bound. She would come to know them, however, all too well.

In November of 1982 Jill and I were blessed with twins, a girl and a boy. We named them Meagan and Brett. To me they were the most beautiful babies ever born. You would think such a blessing would have caused me to change course and to seek the right path. You would think that I would have become the man, the husband, and the father that I should have been. You would think that I would have thrown down the bottle and gotten my life in order.

Instead, I continued to work a retail management job each day and drink each night. Most Sunday mornings I would go to church. Sunday afternoons would be spent with my drinking buddies. I lived a life of duplicity. I remained in a distant land.

In August of 1985 I went into business for myself. My plans were to be a huge success and to be on the cover of Entrepreneur magazine. Nothing could stop me now!

My partner and I would close the business at the end of the day and have our "corporate meetings" at a bar. Jill never knew when to expect me home, but she knew that I would arrive drunk or well on the way.

My partner's wife was also an alcoholic. She wrecked her car twice, received two DUI's, and even spent a weekend in jail. But I was helpless to help her. We would often stop by the neighborhood package store at the same time. Who was I to counsel her on putting her life in order? She died of a hemorrhage one night while asleep.

Again, you would think that this would have shocked me into realizing the thin thread that separates this life from the next. Yet, still I wandered in a distant land.

Shortly after the death of my partner's wife, we sold the business that was supposed to catapult me to fame and fortune. Instead of great wealth, I was left in financial ruins, a reflection of my spiritual condition as well. I had failed once more. The next couple of years would be a continuing search for what the world terms success.

In August of 1988 Jill and I were blessed with another child, a beautiful little girl we named Kellie. You would think . . . But I was abiding in a distant land.

In July of 1989 I began a job that would provide well for my family and give a sense of security. There were Christian co-workers with whom I developed friendships. While around them I put on a display of piety. They did not know my dark secrets of drunken nights and weekends. My life was the definition of duplicity.

My 20-year high school reunion took place in June of 1991. Many of my friends from high school I had not seen since graduation. They remembered me as the young "preacher-boy" who set out with high hopes, dreams, and plans. But that night at the reunion I mingled among my classmates with a drink in my hand, and I partied with the best of them. My antics of the evening left Jill in tears of embarrassment.

Many times during the years of our marriage Jill had pleaded with me to stop drinking. Shortly after the high school reunion episode, however, she sat me down and pleaded more sternly than ever before. She begged me to quit, if not for myself, then for the children and her. She said that she could no longer bear seeing me destroy myself.

Jill did not know of the many mornings I spent looking in the mirror and grimacing at the person I saw. With bloodshot eyes and pounding head, I would wonder why and how? Why did I continue drinking? How had I become this man? It wasn't supposed to turn out this way.

Jill did not know of the many mornings I had determined not to drink for a day. But by the end of the day my resolve to quit was gone, and the string of nights spent drinking continued.

My thoughts while alone during this time began to lead to great despair. I began reflecting on the twenty years that had passed since having my first drink. How could it have been that long? How could I have wasted so many years? This slavery to alcohol wasn't my plan at all. What happened to those dreams that were mine while passing through the gates of Berry College twenty years before?

It seemed to me that the best years of my life were all behind me. It seemed that I was totally helpless to help myself. It seemed that the desire for another drink would forever have me bound. Even my will to live another day seemed in doubt.

Indeed, I was helpless to help myself. Yet, somewhere inside was a memory of a hope I once had, before venturing off into a distant land.

While driving home from work one evening in September of 1991, I didn't make my usual stop by the package store or bar. There was no appetite for dinner when I got home. I went into the darkened bedroom and shut the door behind me.

As I fell down across the bed, twenty years of shame and guilt and regret fell on top of me. **I had finally come to my senses!**

It was as though my heart was broken open, and I began crying out to God as I had never done before. I told him of my sorrow for wasting those twenty years of my life. I told him of my sorrow for shaming him all those years. I told him I no longer wanted my life. I wanted his life for me. I asked for his forgiveness, and I asked for him to take me back and to let me know the closeness of a fellowship with him.

And I asked that he remove all my desire—**all my desire**—ever to drink again.

As I lay on the bed in that darkened room, I began to see images in my mind of many shameful events of the past. What a wasted life I had lived! Again I cried out for God's mercy and forgiveness.

The images of the past ceased and darkness took their place. Then the darkness grew darker still. Although I didn't know what it meant, I knew more than anything that I wanted God to take my existing life with all its darkness and to give me his life with all its hope.

The next moment, **the God of the universe touched me**! I knew his touch from the top of my head, through my body, to the tips of my toes. And the darkness I was seeing before me changed into a pure, white light—no darkness or images from the past—just pure, white light.

As I got up from the bed, I knew beyond any doubt whatsoever that **I had been forgiven! I had been cleansed! And I had been restored back into the fellowship of a relationship I had denied for so many years!** Just like the father of the prodigal son, God had put his arms around me and opened wide the doors and said, **"Welcome Home!"**

It has been over 10 years since that September night in 1991, and what changes have taken place in my life! The desire even for a taste of alcohol has been completely removed from my life. My desire has shifted, instead, to grow closer and to know better the God who is creator of all and yet knows me so personally. He is changing me into his man, as one of his sons. He is, indeed, my heavenly Father.

God has shown himself to me in many ways over the last decade. Allow me to share a recent example.

In late summer of 2001, thirty years after I had passed through the entrance of Berry College as an incoming student, I again passed through those gates with another incoming student—my son, Brett. We both read aloud the words on the low brick wall, "Gate of Opportunity". My impulse was to stop and grab him and shake him—"Son, do you know what this means?"

But I cannot relive my life through the lives of my children. They cannot undo my failures or make right my squandered opportunities. They are God's unique creation, created for his unique plan. Yet, I knew in that moment that God was opening new opportunities for Brett as well as for me. There would be opportunities to pray for my son, to share in his experiences, to encourage him, to be there for him, and to love him as a father loves his son.

As we walked around the campus, a place that held so many memories for me, I knew the work of God's touch. This was a place I thought I could never return without being filled with sadness. Instead, I found myself being filled with **joy** and with **thankfulness** for the way God had so blessed my life!

There is only one explanation for the difference in my life now: **Jesus Christ paid the price for my failures and**

my sins so that I don't have to live a life of shame and guilt and regret. He broke the chains and set me free.

As a child I heard the parable of the Prodigal Son. Never would I have imagined it would be my story.

As a child I sang the great, old hymn, "Amazing Grace". But I didn't really understand what it meant.

Now I know that I am simply a product of **God's Amazing Grace**—nothing more . . . and nothing less.

Part Two

Used By God

CHAPTER 2

MY FAVORITE HAMMER

As Jesus walked beside the Sea of Galilee, he saw Simon and his brother Andrew casting a net into the lake, for they were fishermen. "Come, follow me," Jesus said, "and I will make you fishers of men." At once they left their nets and followed him.

Mark 1: 16–18

One of the most daunting questions we ever ask is this: How do I know that God loves me? We search and long for an answer to that age-old question.

There is, of course, the standard Sunday school answer: "The Bible tells me so . . . For God so loved the world that he gave his one and only Son, that whoever believes in him shall not perish but have eternal life." And that answer, indeed, holds true. But how do I know in a deeply personal way that God really loves ME?

My father had an antique shop and restoration business for several years. During my teenage years and early 20's, I often would help him in the business.

As I watched him work on pieces of furniture, I began to notice a tool that was always present beside him or in his back pocket. It was a small, insignificant-looking hammer with a slim handle and a wedge-shaped head. He would grab it to gently tap a piece of wood into place or to tack a piece of upholstery.

Often, Dad would twirl the little hammer in his hand and comment on how well balanced it was. He frequently would add, "You know, this is my favorite hammer." There is no way to know how many times he picked up that hammer to use on a project or restoration. It was, after all, always near him.

Many years later after my dad had sold the antiques business and had only a small shop in a shed behind his house, I would see the familiar hammer on his workbench. As before, he would pick it up and twirl it in his hand and say, "You know, this is my favorite hammer."

A couple of years ago I was visiting my Dad, and we walked to his workshop. He picked up the hammer like I'd seen him do so many times before. Only this time he handed it to me and said, "I want you to have this hammer. You know, it's . . ."

"I know, Dad, it's your favorite hammer."

It's now my favorite hammer. I look at the stain and varnish and paint on the wooden handle, worn smooth from the many times it was held and used. There's even a thumbprint left in the dried varnish by the one who held and used it.

How does that story relate to the question, "How do I know God loves me?" The answer is simple: I know God loves me, because HE USES ME! He takes a seemingly insignificant life and uses it in his Kingdom. The God who created the universe reaches down and puts the mark of his hand on me, and I become an instrument for his work on earth. My value is shown by the very fact that he has a purpose for me. Jesus showed his love for those first disciples, Simon and Andrew, by putting them to a new work and making them fishers of men.

To know his deep and abiding love, however, we have to be available for his use. As we are available and surrendered to his purpose, he will use us, and we can know the answer to that question in a very personal way. GOD LOVES ME! Therefore, he uses me.

YOUR TURN:

(1) How is God using you at this time?
(2) If you cannot answer the first question specifically, is it because you are not available for his use?
(3) Study examples from the book of Acts. How did God use the early disciples to advance his Kingdom? (Note especially Acts 4:1–13.)
(4) Pray to be more available to be used by God.

CHAPTER 3

A CHRISTMAS TO REMEMBER

So do not fear, for I am with you; do not be dismayed, for I am your God. I will strengthen you and help you; I will uphold you with my righteous right hand.

Isaiah 41:10

It was Christmas, 1983. Jill and I had loaded the car and headed south from Athens to Savannah, Georgia to spend the holiday at Jill's parents' home. Our twins, Meagan and Brett, had recently turned a year old and were in the newly walking mode, which ensured us of exercise. It should have been a joyous time of family celebration and excitement, but the illness of Jill's mom, Mary, during the previous year was a shadow hanging over us that we could not avoid.

Cancer had been found in one of Mary's lungs a year earlier. An operation was performed to remove the lung, but the cancer was discovered to have spread. The surgeons considered any attempts to remove the cancer as futile. Chemotherapy and radiation treatments began, but doctors estimated that she would have a maximum of six months to live.

Mary had outlived the prediction, however, and the cancer for the time being was abated. Nevertheless, the harsh treatments had left her fragile and bed-ridden. Most of the time spent with her that Christmas day was by her bedside. It was difficult for us to see her in that condition.

We began the four-hour trip back to Athens on Christmas night. The roads in South Georgia are long and lonely and never more so than the beginning of that trip. Jill and I just sat in silence as I drove through the dark night. I wondered if we had just spent our last Christmas with Jill's mom, and I knew Jill was wondering the same thing.

Meagan and Brett were in their car seats in the back. An occasional light would illuminate them enough to see their eyes closed in exhausted sleep. About an hour into the trip, that suddenly changed. From the darkness of the back seat, Meagan began singing. I don't mean singing a song, as we normally would think. I don't mean singing a song with intelligible words, or with a particular melody or rhythm. But it was a song. Her voice would strain for the high notes then search for the next note. She was trying to find her range. She was making it up as she went along.

Jill and I began smiling, then laughing as the song continued. And it continued for the next three hours, until we were back home. We were in amazement from the concert we had been given. We had been serenaded by an angel. It was a final gift that Christmas evening, and it will never be forgotten.

I have thought about that night many times, and Jill and I still hold it as one of our most cherished memories. Meagan never repeated another performance like that. How can a masterpiece be improved upon? Out of the despair, sadness, and hopelessness that we were feeling that night, God took a year-old child and used her to bring laughter and joy, to bring encouragement, to bring hope, and to bring a song in a dark night. Can he not use us to bring blessings to others, as well?

How can we bring a blessing to someone today? Usually the first step involves getting out of ourselves. Jesus would phrase it, "DENY YOURSELF". As long as we are consumed by our own problems, perceived needs, wants, or desires, we will be unable to be a blessing to anyone around us. We must put others first by being selfless.

Secondly, we must be available as an instrument in his hand. To do so means that we must remain close to our heavenly Father. Daily quiet times, daily repentance, daily surrender, all are necessary to maintain our fellowship with him.

Also, we must be PURE in our motives. Listen to the words of the Proverb:

All a man's ways seem innocent to him, but motives are weighed by the Lord. (Proverbs 16:2)

We must approach God's work as a little child not seeking self-gain. God is able to use us based on our purity, as illustrated by Paul's words to Timothy:

In a large house there are articles not only of gold and silver, but also of wood and clay; some are for noble purposes and some for ignoble. If a man cleanses himself from the latter, he will be an instrument for noble purposes, made holy, useful to the Master and prepared to do any good work. (2 Timothy 2:20–21)

This passage confirms that with pure motives we are useful to God for noble purposes, and prepared to do any good work.

Furthermore, we must humble ourselves and be willing to do the little things—THE LITTLE THINGS. We like to believe that God is preparing us for some BIG thing, some BIG purpose, and that he will use us in a BIG way. Indeed, he will use us in a big way, but it will be accomplished by doing the little things of the everyday.

Life is composed of the thousands of little things, and in each of those little things are the opportunities to live big. The simple truth is this: Doing all the little things God requires IS the big thing! It may be as simple as carrying a meal to someone in need. It may be sending a card of cheer. It may be saying "thank you" for a kindness. It may be voicing sincere words of encouragement to someone in despair. It may be holding our tongue when someone mistreats us. It may be weeping with someone who mourns. It may be giving a hug or a kiss. It may be singing a song in someone's dark night.

GOD'S BIG PURPOSE is to use us in all the little tasks of our whole life, and it doesn't matter our talents or lack of talents. God used a year-old child. He can use each of us.

Mary shared eleven more Christmas Day's with us. The doctors described her as a miracle, and, indeed, she was. Although bed-ridden and frail for the last years of her life, she touched and blessed the lives of her family and so many others. God used her in a BIG WAY.

YOUR TURN:

(1) Do you find yourself making excuses, rather than making yourself available for God's use?
(2) What "little" things can you do today for your spouse?
(3) What "little" things can you do today for someone who is sick?
(4) What "little" things keep you from living BIG?
(5) Pray that God will show you the "little" tasks for today.

CHAPTER 4

BITE OFF MORE THAN YOU CAN CHEW

When they saw the courage of Peter and John and realized that they were unschooled, ordinary men, they were astonished and they took note that these men had been with Jesus.
Acts 4:13

We've all heard the expression, "Don't bite off more than you can chew." Whether taken literally or figuratively, we've all done it at some time in our life. One literal experience of mine stands out.

In the small town where I grew up, there was a corner restaurant on the downtown square. The official name was "Ye Olde Colonial Restaurant", but everyone called it "Joe's" because of the owner's name, Joe Cunningham. Joe was well known in town as a man who liked to laugh, and he was also known occasionally to play a prank on patrons to get his laugh.

One summer as a teenager I worked in town and would take my lunch hour at Joe's. On each table was a shaker

39

OUT OF A DISTANT LAND

bottle with some kind of long, skinny peppers surrounded by vinegar. Mostly older people seemed to like the juice sprinkled on their turnip greens, and from my observation that was the only purpose they served. Since I hated turnip greens, I had no use for the bottles at all.

During one of my lunches that summer, Joe walked up to my table with his ticket book in hand and, as usual, started writing the total charge for my lunch. He stopped in mid-stroke, however, pointed to the pepper bottle on the table and made a proposition: "If you'll take out one of those peppers and eat the whole thing, lunch is free."

It was an easy decision for me, a working teenager saving for college. "Sure." I reached into the bottle and picked out one of those long, skinny peppers, put it all the way into my mouth, and bit down on the entire length up to the stem. Two chomps later I was spitting it out in a state of panic. I was absolutely sure my mouth was on fire. Smoke was certainly coming out my ears. Sweat poured from my forehead and the back of my neck. The pitcher of tea on the table was consumed in record time. Finally after thirty minutes of coughing and gasping and gulping iced tea, I decided that I would live to see another day.

The end of the story is simple. Joe got his best laugh of the week, and I paid for my lunch. I had "bitten off more than I could chew" (I'm reminded also of another expression—"There ain't no such thing as a free lunch").

One simple plea of Jabez in his prayer (made known to many by the recent book by Bruce Wilkerson) was for God to "enlarge my territory". That can be interpreted: "Allow me to bite off more than I can chew."

That goes against the grain of what most of us desire today. We use the expressions, "my plate is already full" or "I have too many irons in the fire" or "I'm busier than a June bug in a chicken coup". The last thing we want is more responsibilities or demands for our time.

But suppose we take the risk and pray such a prayer and God allows us to bite off more than we can chew. First, we may feel overwhelmed. We begin saying, "I just can't do this, Lord." And that's exactly what God desires; for us to realize that we can't do it, but that he can through us. Suddenly we're forced to rely on him instead of our own limited abilities and resources.

Secondly, we discover a new set of priorities. We begin to realize that so many of the "urgent" things in the day-to-day routine really don't matter.

In Acts 4, we read of Peter and John going around preaching and healing, and the religious powers of the time were not pleased. The two disciples were brought before the Sanhedrin—the rulers, elders, and teachers of the law—and asked to account for their actions.

Clearly Peter and John had bitten off more than they could chew. Yet with boldness, courage, and the filling of the Holy Spirit, they proclaimed the truth of Salvation through Jesus Christ. The men of the Sanhedrin were "astonished and they took note that these men had been with Jesus".

The lesson of the story is simple. God takes ordinary people, who are willing to bite off more than they can chew, and does extraordinary things.

YOUR TURN:

(1) Are you presently in a spiritual comfort zone?
(2) When was the last time you "stretched" yourself beyond your own capabilities?
(3) How do we limit the Kingdom of God by doing only what is comfortable for us?
(4) Commit to "biting off more than you can chew". Pray that God will provide such an opportunity.
(5) For further related reading: "If You Want to Walk on Water, You've Got to Get Out of the Boat" by John Ortberg.

Part Three

Share The Good News

CHAPTER 5

FREE INDEED

If you hold to my teaching, you are really my disciples. Then you will know the truth, and the truth will set you free.

John 8:31–32

Have you ever known the confines of a prison? Most of us have never been locked up as a prisoner, but we may have visited a prison or been part of a prison ministry. Maybe we have been in a situation that seemed like a prison.

Have you ever been in the military? To some a term in a branch of the military may seem like a prison. As a member of the armed services you are committed to a time period of service, and you can't just walk away. I spent four years in the Air Force, and I'll never forget my thought as I drove off base for the last time—I'M FREE!

Each day there are those around us living in their own prison. They are captives as surely as someone chained in the darkest dungeon. An invisible captor named sin holds them. Sin has so entangled and ensnared them that try as they might, they cannot escape the grip.

Last week a co-worker of mine came back to work after an absence of five weeks. It was no secret why he'd been gone. He had undergone treatment for alcoholism.

For twenty-five years this man had been a prisoner of the bottle. For twelve years I had worked beside him and never known of his chains. But when I saw him last Friday, he was a free man. His chains had been broken not by the treatment program, but by the one who breaks the power of sin and sets the captive free, the person of Jesus Christ.

Several of us at work join together each morning to pray. This new brother in Christ joined us Friday, and as we held hands we celebrated, because we had all once been prisoners but were now free—FREE INDEED!

We should look around us each day and be aware that a prisoner may be right beside us, wearing the chains of guilt and sin. We should listen to the Holy Spirit's still, small voice speaking of the needs of someone near us. We should tell the Good News—we don't have to be prisoners of sin and shame. Although we cannot free others or free ourselves, we know and can lead others to the one who is the great emancipator.

> *How can you say that we shall be set free?*
> *Jesus replied, "I tell you the truth, everyone who sins is a slave to sin. Now a slave has no permanent place in the family, but a son belongs to it forever. So if the Son sets you free, you will be free indeed." (John 8:33–36)*

YOUR TURN:

(1) Has the Holy Spirit impressed upon you the need to speak to someone at work who may be chained to sin?
(2) Celebrate FREEDOM DAY today.
(3) Pray that you will be sensitive to others who may be in bondage.

CHAPTER 6

THE PERFECT GIFT

Magi from the east came to Jerusalem and asked, "Where is the one who has been born king of the Jews? We saw his star in the east and have come to worship him."

On coming to the house, they saw the child with his mother Mary, and they bowed down and worshiped him. Then they opened their treasures and presented him with gifts of gold and of incense and of myrrh.

Matthew 2:1–2, 11

Antique auctions are a favorite pastime for my wife and me. Recently we purchased an old framed print of the Magi, the three wise men, seated on their camels overlooking the little town of Bethlehem with the bright star shining in the night sky.

This print reminded me of a message used on many Christmas cards: "Wise men still seek him."

When we paid for our purchase at the auction, we were given a receipt with the cost and a description of the item.

This was the description of the Magi print: "Picture of men on horses". Maybe that's what horses look like in that part of Georgia (it's been said, after all, that camels are horses that a Baptist committee put together). Reading that description reminded me that there are still those who do not know the Christ.

We who know him look at the picture of the wise men with different eyes. We see the star as the guiding light. It was the light that led the wise men to God's greatest gift to man. However, the greatest gift is not the Jesus of Bethlehem. Rather, the greatest gift is the Jesus of Calvary.

Jesus did not come to give us Christmas. He came as the LAMB OF GOD. He came for THE FORGIVENESS OF SIN. He came so that we might know ABUNDANT LIFE. He came to give us ETERNAL LIFE.

We think of Christmas as a time of presenting gifts. The Magi laid down their gifts to the Christ child at Bethlehem. Do we think of Easter as a time of presenting gifts? Jesus laid down his life for us at Calvary. His was the perfect gift.

I'm reminded of the inscription from another Christmas card: "He came to pay a debt he did not owe, to free us of a debt we could never pay."

YOUR TURN:

(1) Why is Christmas a more "popular" holiday than Easter?
(2) What holds more significance, the manger or the cross?

(3) Which involves more commitment, the manger or the cross?
(4) Pray that God will reveal to you his perfect gift.

Part Four

Growth—A Daily Choice

CHAPTER 7

LIKE A TREE

And I pray that you, being rooted and established in love, may have power, together with all the saints, to grasp how wide and long and high and deep is the love of Christ.
Ephesians 3:17–18

As I'm hiking along a trail or making my way up a mountain stream while fishing, I'm drawn to the individual trees along the way. I have always enjoyed looking at trees and admiring their characteristics and beauty. One of the perennial projects of science class or Cub Scout merit badges always included the identification of trees.

When I examine a tree I notice the texture of the bark, the straightness or crookedness of the trunk, the shape and color of the leaves, the scars left from brutal weather of the past, and the spread of its canopy of branches. Just like each of us, trees have similar characteristics. Yet, each is unique.

There is a particular characteristic of trees that I've also noticed and admired—trees **just keep on growing till they die**. It is a quality not possessed by us. We do grow physically for the first quarter or so of our life span, but then we stop growing for the most part (except for horizontal fluctuations).

Many times I have observed trees that have been blown over by the wind. Even so, part of the root system still extends into the source of life, and the tree adjusts to this new circumstance. The limbs on the skyward side begin growing toward the sun's light. The tree doesn't know its awkward, unnatural condition and keeps on growing till it dies.

When we are born again as Christians, there is no assurance that we will grow at all. We accept our "new life" in Christ without the discipline to grow more Christ-like. Perhaps tragedies or other storms of life have toppled us, and our roots were not deep nor were they tapped into the Source of life. Many Christians wander aimlessly for years with no change in their spiritual stature. That is not God's design. He wants us to be like a tree and keep growing till we die.

Often I have seen trees appearing to grow out of solid rock. How is it possible for them to live, to stand upright, and to grow in such a condition? The answer lies in the roots, which wind around the rocks and through the crevices and thrust deeply into the ground to the springs of life. These trees even use the rocks as a solid platform on which to stand and grow.

Sadly, we as Christians often use our own external conditions to justify dormancy. Perhaps there are obstacles that seem to us like boulders, and we use them as excuses for our lack of growth. Our life does not follow God's desire for us to know the full measure of his purpose.

We should be more like a tree. Our roots should sink deep into the Source, our Creator. Our limbs should reach out to embrace the purpose for which we were created. And we should grow upward as we

> *"Press on toward the goal to win the prize for which god has called me heavenward in Christ Jesus." (Philippians 3:14)*

We should be more like a tree and **just keep on growing till we die**.

YOUR TURN:

(1) How would you rate your Christian growth over the past five years?
(2) What year do you believe was your greatest spiritual growth spurt?
(3) Rings on a cut tree reveal what years were good growth years and what years were droughts. What will your "ring" look like for this year?
(4) Will you commit to growth by spending time daily before the Lord (our source of life and growth)?
(5) Pray that your roots will grow deeper into Him.

CHAPTER 8

LIGHT POST TO LIGHT POST

Your word is a lamp to my feet and a light for my path.
Psalms 119:105

When I started running for fun at age 15, little did I know that I would still be running "for fun" in my late 40's. I'm still exploring for exercise that is more fun and easier on the joints.

One of my present fun running routes takes me through my neighborhood. At a point about halfway, I round a corner onto another street. Dread overtakes me at that spot. All I see ahead is a mile-long stretch of steady uphill pavement. As I suck in more wind, I begin the battle with gravity. Finally, the high mark is reached, and I turn onto another street that offers a flat course. By then I'm huffing and puffing from the previous mile, and it takes a little while to recover and find the energy to regain my stride.

When the time changed back to Eastern Standard Time in autumn, I found myself running the neighborhood route in the dark. As I rounded the turn that put me on the uphill street, my view was only about 100 feet—just the distance illuminated by the light post on the corner. When the light from that light post faded, another light would begin to share its glow. This continued for the mile length of the uphill street, until I reached the high point and turned onto the next flat street along the route. Suddenly I realized something unusual. I wasn't huffing and puffing, and I continued full of energy without breaking stride.

Why didn't I have the usual weariness at this point? As I considered this question, the answer became obvious to me. When it had been daylight, I could see the entire stretch of that uphill street. It seemed daunting, and, in many ways, I was weary before the uphill trudging began. The experience on this day's run was different, because I could only see about 100 feet at a time, and then another 100 feet, and then another. Each short stretch was done without dread of what lay ahead. When the entire stretch was completed, I found myself not weary, but energized for the rest of the course.

Many times I notice people as they arrive at their job at the beginning of the workday. A look of defeat is etched on their face. They are already imagining the load of tasks that awaits them. They only see the long, uphill struggle. They are weary before the workday even begins. The day becomes drudgery, lacking in energy or enthusiasm.

This trait of human nature manifests itself in other ways. We envision the tasks that lay before us, not only at work, but also in such jobs as the raising of our children. We are concerned with meeting the financial needs of a growing family. We realize the responsibility of setting a Godly example before others. The demands of living the Christian life seem overwhelming. A devastating illness may have given life a different perspective.

Perhaps the most wearisome of all, however, are the uncertainties of life—the things we cannot see. What lies ahead that we do not know? What is beyond the bend in the course?

A friend once said to me, "I'm not content just to see the next step, I want to know the end!" If we are honest with ourselves, we probably identify with and add to such a confession. "Lord, I want to know how my life turns out! I want to know the course of my children's lives!" We're not content, to use a football analogy, of running a play at a time—we want to know the final score!

The Psalmist writes:

Your word is a lamp to my feet and a light for my path.
(Psalms 119:105)

God doesn't give us knowledge or sight of the ending. We do not know all the bends or all the hills we may encounter. He does not shine a beacon to illuminate the next six months or a year ahead. Life is so uncertain. Why is he not more help?

Look back on the course your life has already taken. Maybe you see some difficult times of struggle. Financial hardships litter the roadside. Challenges with children come to mind. Illnesses and death of loved ones have been segments of the journey. What if you had been able to see all of this before it occurred? Would there have been a weariness of heart? Yet, somehow God granted endurance for each challenge as it came along.

Perhaps the period we face at this moment finds us in an uphill struggle. We want to know what lies at the top. When will it get easier?

The truth is simply this: God provides a lamp for our feet (that take only a step at a time) and a light for our path (that lies directly in front of us).

We cannot know all the details or methods that God will use in our life or the exact course on which he will lead us. One thing we can know, however: God empowers us **one moment at a time**. When he tells us "his grace is sufficient", he assures us it is sufficient for each moment—a moment at a time.

When Jesus tells us as disciples, "My yoke is easy and my burden is light", he is speaking of every aspect of the Christian walk—including our desire to know the future and our fear of it. Since he is sharing our burden, he is making it possible to bear each moment—a moment at a time.

Jesus said:

"Come to me, all you who are weary and burdened, and I will give you rest. Take my yoke upon you and learn from me, for I am gentle and humble in heart, and you will find

rest for your souls. For my yoke is easy and my burden is light." (Matthew 11:28–30)

YOUR TURN:

(1) Do you often feel overwhelmed?
(2) Do you have anxiety about what may happen in the future?
(3) Notice Jesus' words: "Take my yoke upon you and learn from me." What can we learn from him to help us endure the "uphill's" that are bound to come?
(4) Pray that God will give you the grace for just that very next step.

CHAPTER 9

THE FULL MOON

And we, who with unveiled faces all reflect the Lord's glory, are being transformed into his likeness with ever-increasing glory, which comes from the Lord, who is the Spirit.
2 Corinthians 3:18

Of all the sights that we witness, there are few more awe-inspiring than seeing the sun set in the west as the moon is rising in the east. On the one horizon is the fiery, brilliant orb of the sun, while on the other horizon is the soft, textured glow of the moon that is "full".

While observing this occurrence recently, I remembered what I had learned about the moon in early school years. First, I recalled that the source of the moon's light is not from itself. Rather, the moon's light is a reflection of light from the sun.

Then I recalled why the moon has its different phases. The moon does not always reflect the same amount of light from the sun for one simple reason: the world gets in the way. There is even a time each month when the moon reflects no light at all. At that time the world is completely blocking the light from the sun.

Our Christian life can be compared to the moon. Our light source is not of ourselves, it is from the Son—S-O-N. We must reflect Jesus Christ alone if we are to give light to those living in darkness.

We do not always reflect that light, however, and the reason is simple: **The world gets in the way**. The world distracts us, hinders us, lures us, and makes us its own. The world blocks out the light from a radiant SON, and others do not see the light of Christ in us.

There is a further resemblance of the moon with the Christian life. Think again on what we learned about the moon's phases and recall that the moon is either "waning" or "waxing".

The moon is waning when each day more and more of the world gets in the way of the sun's light, and the moon becomes increasingly dark. The Christian's spiritual life is likewise waning when more and more of the world is getting in the way of the SON's light, and less of Christ is being reflected.

The moon is waxing when each day the shadow of the world recedes a little more and the moon grows toward fullness when the sun's light is unhindered. The Christian's spiritual life is waxing when each day a little more of the world is shrugged off, and we move toward the time when the SON's light is reflected in fullness.

We may tend to ask what phase of reflection we are in now. The more important question is this: Are we "waning", or are we "waxing"?

YOUR TURN:

(1) Answer the last question posed?
(2) What in the world is blocking the light of Christ in your life?
(3) Listen to or read the words of the chorus, "Turn Your Eyes Upon Jesus".
(4) Please read 2 Corinthians 3:18.
(5) Pray that God will help you remove a little more of the world today.

Part Five

Live It Now

CHAPTER 10

WHAT WOULD IT LOOK LIKE

What is your life? You are a mist that appears for a little while and then vanishes. Instead, you ought to say, "If it is the Lord's will, we will live and do this or that." As it is you boast and brag. All such boasting is evil. Anyone, then, who knows the good he ought to do and doesn't do it, sins.
James 4:14–17

What do you do when you want to sell a vehicle? You probably do what I recently did to a 32-year old truck that was originally purchased by my grandfather. You fix it up! You repair the things that are broken. You wash and wax the outside. You clean out the dash and under the seats and find half-eaten peanut butter and jelly sandwiches and cookie crumbs.

What do you do when you want to sell your house? You fix the drippy faucet and patch the hole in the wall where the picture was never hung. You paint outside and inside. You mow and trim more meticulously than you ever did before. You may even pressure wash the walkway and driveway. Why? Because you want the buyer to believe it's worth the price he's paying.

After all the hard work of getting that vehicle or house ready to sell, you stand back and admire it and ask yourself, "Why didn't I do this long ago so that I could have enjoyed it all this time?" Finally you've gotten things the way you want them, the way they should be.

Why do we wait? Primarily, we wait because we have no sense of urgency. There's always tomorrow. We just don't get around to it, "too busy, ya' know".

Unfortunately, this inclination carries over into other aspects of our life, especially our spiritual life. We lack a sense of urgency. After all, we're going to live to be 100. There's plenty of time. But James reminds us, our life is but a "mist".

Over a year ago I had a question posed to me: "If your life were exactly as it should be, what would it look like?" That's a tough question. It demands that we examine our life, and examine our relationships with others and with God. It causes us to realize what needs to be added, or what needs to be taken away. We begin to see the idols and discover the hindrances.

Last week I finally wrote the answer to that question as it applies to different aspects of my life. I am ashamed that it took me so long. Again I'm reminded of the words of James: "Anyone who knows the good he ought to do and doesn't do it, sins." I'm also reminded of the words spoken by my father when I was in my early 20's: "The worst state that a man can be, is knowing what to do and not doing it."

How many of us will look back on our life in regret and say; "Why didn't I submit to God's plan long ago and experience all the full, abundant life he intended?" Sadly, many will never have that sense of urgency—or get around to it, "too busy, ya' know". Yet, we should seek to be worthy followers, and our life should exemplify the price that Jesus paid for it. Life means too much to waste it!

If your life were exactly as it should be, what would it look like?

YOUR TURN:

(1) Answer the question posed above. Break it down into these five categories:
   A. FAMILY
   B. WORK
   C. RENEWAL
   D. OTHER SERVICE
   E. CHURCH
(2) Use this exercise as a foundation upon which to build.
(3) Pray that God will give you clarity in determining what your life should look like.

CHAPTER 11

TUIT

But encourage one another daily, as long as it is called To-day.

Hebrews 3:13

A friend recently gave me something that I've needed for a long time. It will open many doors for me and allow me to be much more productive in my life. It's a little round disc a couple of inches across with one word written on it: TUIT.

All those sticky doors in our house, the room that needs painting, the "honey-do" list of several pages—all this can now be accomplished. I've finally gotten a round TUIT!

Is anyone not guilty of it? Maybe I'd better wait until tomorrow to even mention it. No, I've gotten a round TUIT, so I can go ahead and say it—**Procrastination**. Is anyone not guilty of its delaying tactics?

Little chores and tasks we seem to always put off are one thing, but the more important duties of life we also tend to surrender to procrastination. It shouldn't be the way of the Christian. Procrastination contradicts the discipline we are to exhibit as disciples.

My junior year in high school was a year of rebellion to schoolwork. I went through that "what good is trigonometry going to do me in life" stage. My grades in previous years had been all A's, but at the end of the junior year I had a low B average.

During the period we chose classes for the senior year, the high school principal came by the classroom and sat in a desk beside me. I knew Mr. Riden very well. He and my Dad were both deacons in the church. I liked and respected him.

Mr. Riden looked over my choices for the upcoming year. He also looked over my grades for the current year. Getting up from the desk, he patted me on the back and said, "Gary, you're under-achieving by ten points." There was nothing I could say in my defense. He had to say nothing else and walked from the room.

The encounter left me ashamed. I knew he was right, and I determined in that moment that my senior year would be different. I would do my best in the year to come.

Many times in the years since my high school days I've wanted to tell Mr. Riden how much he meant to me as my principal. I've wanted to tell him how he challenged me to do my best, and what a difference it made when the time came to select a college. I just wanted to say, "Thank you."

This past week Mr. Riden died. The days and weeks of procrastination had turned into twenty-five years, and now it is too late. My opportunities are gone.

We read the account in Luke 17 of Jesus' meeting ten men with leprosy. He healed all ten, but only one, a Samaritan, came back to say "thank you". The others may have counted on having the opportunity later. Jesus asked, "Were not all ten cleansed? Where are the other nine? Was no one found to return and give praise to God except this foreigner?" Most of us probably read this story as a lesson in gratitude, but I believe it is also a lesson in procrastination. The other nine men were, no doubt, grateful. They just probably figured there would be plenty of time for gratitude later—tomorrow, perhaps . . . or next week.

How many times have we not said the "thank you" that needed to be said? Was it because of ingratitude or because of thoughtlessness? Or was it because we just planned to say it later? And it was never said. We need to show our appreciation to others—**Today**.

We see those around us with physical needs. They may be hungry, sick, or cold. They may be slaves to addictions. They need our help—**Today**.

There are those who we have wronged or hurt. We should ask their forgiveness—**Today**. There are those who have wronged or hurt us. We should forgive them—before they ask—**Today**.

There are those close to us, perhaps in our own family, who need to hear the heart-felt words "I love you." Say it—**Today**.

Too much we put off because we never get "around to it". We even put off answering Christ's call to follow him. When Jesus calls us to any service, answer him—**Today**.

YOUR TURN:

(1) List two procrastinations of the last 24 hours.
(2) Is there a present need of asking forgiveness? Extending forgiveness?
(3) Is there a "thank you" card you need to send?
(4) Is there a card of encouragement you need to send?
(5) Pray that God will point out to you the things that need doing today.

Part Six

Hard To Be Humble

CHAPTER 12

HOW WE FORGET

"God, have mercy on me, a sinner."

Luke 18:13

Most of us know an ex-smoker who kicked the habit and now is an anti-smoking militant. These soldiers rant and rave over anyone who dares light up a cigarette in front of them. They condemn smokers as ignorant people who are destroying their bodies and infringing on the rights of those around them. How soon they forget that they once were smokers.

There was a hit song during the time of the so-called Jesus Freaks, about 1970, titled, "Spirit in the Sky." I don't know who wrote it or why it was written, unless it was someone's spoof on the Jesus Freaks. Some of the words were, "Never been a sinner, never sinned . . .".

Do we believe as Christians that we have "never been a sinner"? How soon we forget our life before Christ. And how soon we forget our present weaknesses and failings.

It has been said that there are only two kinds of people: the sinners who consider themselves righteous, and the righteous who consider themselves sinners. Jesus illustrated this in a parable found in the book of Luke:

> *To some who were confident of their own righteousness and looked down on everybody else, Jesus told this parable:* "*Two men went up to the temple to pray, one a Pharisee and the other a tax collector. The Pharisee stood up and prayed about himself: 'God, I thank you that I am not like other men—robbers, evildoers, adulterers—or even like this tax collector. I fast twice a week and give a tenth of all I get.'*
>
> "*But the tax collector stood at a distance. He would not even look up to heaven, but beat his breast and said, 'God, have mercy on me, a sinner.'*
>
> "*I tell you that this man, rather than the other, went home justified before God.*"
> (Luke 18:9–14)

How soon we forget who we were before Christ transformed us and made us a new creation. We rant and rave in our "righteousness" about the heathens, the pagans, the sinners—the drunks, the druggies, the prostitutes—**the sinners**.

But the Apostle Paul remembered and even called himself "chief sinner". He remembered doing all he could to oppose the name of Jesus of Nazareth. He remembered putting many saints in prison and casting his vote for their death.

Yet, his life reflected the prayer of the tax collector: "God, have mercy on me, a sinner." And he met his Lord justified.

How soon we forget that we did not change ourselves. God changed us through Jesus Christ.

Jesus concluded the parable of the Pharisee and the tax collector with this truth:

"For everyone who exalts himself will be humbled, and he who humbles himself will be exalted."

YOUR TURN:

(1) What is your definition of a hypocrite?
(2) In any way do you fit the definition?
(3) Think of the things for which you most criticize others.
(4) Please read Matthew 7:1–5. These are stern words of Jesus. Do you have a plank in your eye when you criticize someone else?
(5) Pray that God will make us see who we would be without him.

CHAPTER 13

I AM THE MAN

Pride goes before destruction, a haughty spirit before a fall.
Proverbs 16:18

It is called "talking trash". We hear it before sporting events, especially football. Players and coaches have press conferences in which boastfulness and an "in your face" attitude prevail. Big claims are made about the superiority of one player or team over the other.

This attitude carries over onto the football field on game day. At the end of practically every play, the player who considers himself the hero on that particular play will jump up from the ground and begin his "strut". He may lift his hands in the air or use them to point to himself. What he is really saying and wishing to convey is this:

I AM THE MAN!

His teammates often join the celebration and strut around him or slap his shoulder pads or helmet. What they are really saying and wishing to convey is this:

YEAH! YOU ARE THE MAN!

Can you hear the whisper of the proverb, "Pride goes before destruction . . ."?

A well-known story in the Bible, found in 2 Samuel 11, portrays this prideful attitude well. It involves THE MAN, King David. He was a man who knew God's favor. He had been protected and blessed beyond measure for his faithfulness to God. He had many fans and followers in his kingdom. He had slain the Philistine champion, Goliath. He had known victory after victory on the battlefield. His subjects had long cheered, "Saul has slain his thousands, and David his tens of thousands". Perhaps all this was too much to expect David to remain humble. Perhaps he came to a point where he began to believe,

I AM THE MAN!

David decided one spring to send Joab off to fight his wars while he remained in his palace in Jerusalem. One night from the roof of his palace David saw a beautiful woman bathing. He was filled, even consumed, with desire for her. And he could have her. After all, he was the king. He was THE MAN!

David sent for this woman, Bathsheba, and slept with her, and she became pregnant. The scheming began. David wanted to have Bathsheba for his own, but Bathsheba's husband, Uriah, was a real obstacle. (Uriah, by the way, was a warrior fighting in the battles for David.) But since David was THE MAN, he arranged for Joab to place Uriah in a position on the battlefield where death was certain. The plan worked. Uriah was out of the way, and David had Bathsheba for his own. They were married, and she bore him a son.

David was probably doing some pretty powerful strutting about this time. Certainly he was very proud of what he had accomplished. He probably walked the corridors of the palace, with jutting chest and jabbing fingers toward himself, proclaiming,

I AM THE MAN!

The Bible proclaims, however,

But the thing David had done displeased the Lord. (2 Samuel 11:27)

So the Lord gave the prophet, Nathan, a divine appointment to share a story with David.

When Nathan came to him, he said, "There were two men in a certain town, one rich and the other poor. The rich man had a very large number of sheep and cattle, but the poor man had nothing except one little ewe lamb he had bought. He raised it, and it grew up with him and his children. It shared his food, drank from his cup and even slept in his arms. It was like a daughter to him.

"Now a traveler came to the rich man, but the rich man refrained from taking one of his own sheep or cattle to prepare a meal for the traveler who had come to him. Instead, he took the ewe lamb that belonged to the poor man and prepared it for the one who had come to him."

David burned with anger against the man and said to Nathan, "As surely as the Lord lives, the man who did this deserves to die! He must pay for that lamb four times over, because he did such a thing and had no pity."

Then Nathan said to David, "YOU ARE THE MAN!" (2 Samuel 12:1–7)

If each of us only had a Nathan, what a different view we might have of ourselves. David had thought he was top of the heap, king of the hill, and God's chosen one who could do no wrong. But when Nathan pointed his finger at David and said, "YOU ARE THE MAN!" Nathan was pointing at a man who had committed the most grievous sins.

In that moment David saw himself as God saw him, and he suffered harsh consequences for his actions. Gladly, however, David's heart belonged to the Lord, and his prayer of repentance is the 51st Psalms.

> *Against you, you only, have I sinned . . .*
> *Create in me a pure heart, O God,*
> *and renew a steadfast spirit within me . . .*
> *Restore to me the joy of your salvation*
> *and grant me a willing spirit, to sustain me . . .*
> *The sacrifices of God are a broken spirit;*
> *a broken and contrite heart*

Hard To Be Humble

O God, you will not despise.
Wash away all my iniquity
and cleanse me from my sin . . .
(Psalms 51:2,4,10,12,17)

We, also, must see ourselves as God sees us. Perhaps we are not fortunate enough to know a Nathan, but our times of prayerful self-examination should reveal the sin that persists in our lives. Pride is a sin. It is a deadly sin that leads to many other sins. We must be aware of the warning signs of excessive pride.

When we start believing we are superior, when we find ourselves strutting around with the attitude of, I AM THE MAN, then we should fall to our knees as the repentant David, who saw himself a sinner and prayed,

Have mercy on me, O God, according to your unfailing love.
(Psalms 51:1)

Let our new proclamation be:

I AM GOD'S MAN!

YOUR TURN:

(1) Is "in your face" pride rampant in our society?
(2) Do you have feelings of superiority at work? Do you believe yourself to be better than your co-workers?

(3) Do you feel more pious than others at church?
(4) Are you seeing the warning signs of pride?
(5) Pray for repentance in the area of your pride.

Part Seven

Buzzwords

CHAPTER 14

RIGHTS

But I have not used any of these rights.
1 Corinthians 9:15

He has been a tireless civil rights crusader. His face has been on television news shows and in newspapers for many years. He has done many good works in support of his cause. However, he has a weakness that has placed him in the news for a different reason. He often has too much alcohol to drink and then attempts to drive his car.

Several times he has been arrested for reckless driving and driving under the influence of alcohol. Each time, this civil rights legend expresses outrage that he has received this kind of harassment. He claims his arrest is strictly politically motivated and intended to embarrass him.

Recently his outrage from being arrested took a new twist. In a news conference he was adamant in his own defense. This champion of rights boldly proclaimed, "It's my Constitutional **right** to drive a car!"

While in college I took a course or two in Constitutional law. Furthermore, I have read the U.S. Constitution with all of its amendments, and I do not recall "driving a car" listed as one of our "rights" as citizens (perhaps a recent amendment was added of which I am not aware).

It is, unquestionably, one of the most popular words in our society today—**Rights**. It is heard in every circle and among every group. From each of these groups the cry is heard, "You have no **right** to step on **my rights**!" The Founding Fathers themselves understood the difficulty of ratifying the Constitution without the addition of the Bill of Rights.

Think of how many times the word is mentioned in reference to specific causes: civil rights, abortion rights, rights of the unborn, animal rights, woman's right to choose, patients' bill of rights, victim's rights, gay rights, equal rights amendment, father's rights, women's rights, reproductive rights. The list could continue for several pages. We are a people obsessed with our "rights".

What should be our attitude toward "rights" as citizens? John Calvin said, "Does a person demand his rights? Certainly, I am prepared to grant him his rights, but in so doing I shall say that he has no other rights than the rights to fulfill his duties." Doesn't that statement lead to an entirely different view of rights?

Buzzwords

Imagine for a moment that a politician began campaigning on a platform compelling us as citizens to be more diligent in accepting our duties and responsibilities and to quit whining about our rights. How many people would be anxious to jump on this politician's bandwagon?

Imagine for a moment that the old-fashioned civics books were reintroduced into the school systems. A friend recently gave me a book titled, *The Good Citizen's Handbook; A Guide to Proper Behavior*. It is a compilation of duties, responsibilities, and character traits required for good citizenship culled from civics texts, citizenship manuals, government pamphlets, and scouting manuals from the 1920's to 1960's. The topics include: a good citizen is worthy, a good citizen is fit, a good citizen controls himself, be a good family member, good workmanship, and what you owe the community. Sadly, most who read such material today would only find the subjects humorous, out of date, and "corny". "Rights" are most important—not duties.

What should be our attitude toward "rights" as Christians (citizens of heaven)? We are told to make our attitude the attitude of Christ (Philippians 2:5). A few examples from the Gospel should tell of Christ's attitude toward his rights.

Consider, first, what rights Christ should have enjoyed on earth. He is, after all, the Son of God sent down from the glory of heaven. He is, after all, the Lord of all creation. With these credentials he should have had all rights afforded to the King of Kings. Instead, he forfeited all those rights for one purpose—to do the **will** of the Father (duty).

Consider his final hours before the Cross. Jesus had finished the evening meal with his disciples. It should have been a time when he accepted the accolades due him. Instead, he wrapped a towel around his waist and washed his disciples' feet. It was one of Christ's greatest lessons to his disciples.

> "Now that I, your Lord and Teacher, have washed your feet, you also should wash one another's feet. I have set you an example that you should do as I have done for you." (John 13:14–15)

Not demanding his rights, he became a humble servant.

Later that evening, knowing what awaited him the next day, Jesus prayed on the Mount of Olives. He could have called ten thousand angels, but this is his prayer:

> "Father, if you are willing, take this cup from me; yet not my will, but yours be done." (Luke 22:42)

Not claiming his rights, he became a sacrifice for all.

Jesus was arrested following his prayer by a group of his enemies and did not resist. He could have waved his hand and stricken them all dead. Instead, he used his hand to heal the Roman soldier's ear cut off by a follower. He went quietly before Pilate, who asked,

> Are you the king of the Jews?
> Jesus replied, "Yes, it is as you say."
> The chief priests accused him of many things. So again Pilate asked him,
> Aren't you going to answer? See how many things they are accusing you of.

But Jesus made no reply, and Pilate was amazed. (Mark 15:2–5)

Pilate knew something was different about Jesus. Pilate was amazed, because Jesus did not invoke his rights.

Jesus **willingly** forfeited his rights to do the will of the Father. Whether in the washing of his disciples' feet or the shedding of his own blood, Jesus never claimed his rights as the Son of God.

He bids us follow him. He bids us follow his example.
"I have set you an example that you should do as I have done for you."
He asks to be Lord of our life, and that means surrendering our **all** to him—that includes **our rights**.

YOUR TURN:

(1) Please read 1 Corinthians 9:14–19. Does Paul set a Christ-like example?
(2) How often do you invoke your rights?
(3) How difficult is it for you to remain silent when others are stepping on what you perceive to be your rights?
(4) How are the forfeiture of rights and humility related?
(5) Pray that God will help you surrender what you may consider your precious rights.

CHAPTER 15

MODERATION

When tempted, no one should say, "God is tempting me." For God cannot be tempted by evil, nor does he tempt anyone; but each one is tempted when, by his own evil desire, he is dragged away and enticed.

James 1:13–14

On the official seal of the State of Georgia is an arch supported by columns. Intertwined within the columns is a banner with three words: **Wisdom**, **Justice**, and **Moderation**. "Wisdom" and "Justice" are understandable values for a state government, but I am not sure about the ideal of moderation. Perhaps it is simply a call for constraint from extremes in the arena of governance. But who defines extremes? Let's leave it to the political scientists to define the word "moderation" as it applies to government and look at other applications of the word that fall into more daily usage.

Moderation is another popular "buzzword" and mindset of our culture. Often it is used in connection with our physical well-being. We are told that vitamins and other health supplements should be taken "in moderation". The adage, "if two vitamins are good for you, then six must be three times better", is cited as wrong thinking. Moderation is the key. The same may be said of physical exercise. Over exertion could cause injury or damage to our body, while lethargy leads to obesity and overall poor health. A fine balance exists between our nutrition and exercise. Moderation is the fulcrum upon which these two rests.

The mindset of moderation goes beyond the rational need to balance our physical health, however. It is used as a justification for certain behavior. Actions are said to be acceptable as long as they are done "in moderation". Of concern to the Christian should be the application of moderation to justify or excuse sin. Consider the following examples to illustrate this point.

Gambling to most Christians is considered a sin. It does not fit into the pattern of stewardship of the possessions that God has entrusted us. Yet, we excuse or justify betting on a ball game every now and then, or we buy a few lottery tickets when the jackpot gets too tempting to resist. Perhaps we even include vacation trips to Las Vegas or other casino locations. Our justification sounds something like this: "It's just a little innocent fun. I'm not spending the grocery money, after all. I'm just doing a little betting . . . in **moderation**."

The drinking of alcoholic beverages by Christians is a common practice justified by the moderation claim. The rationale may follow this line: "I'm mostly a social drinker;

dinner parties, after work drinks with business associates, and a few beers watching a ball game. It's not like I'm an alcoholic, after all. What could be wrong with drinking . . . **in moderation?**"

Some Christians may even justify the viewing of pornography, whether it is from web sites, adult movies, or magazines. The reasoning insists: "It's really a 'victimless' thing. I'm the only one affected, and I've got it under control—no harm done. It's not the real hard-core stuff, after all, just a pleasurable thing done . . . **in moderation.**"

Of course, in our piety, we do not try to justify sins with "victims". We will readily agree that adultery, murder, and theft are not acceptable practices, even in moderation.

What is wrong with using the moderation excuse for this kind of behavior? Notice I used the word "behavior", because we, at this stage, quit viewing it as sin. We begin to believe that it only becomes sin when it is taken to some level that we call extreme. The compulsive gambler is a sinner. The alcoholic is a sinner. The person with an obsession for pornography is a sinner. We, who can keep sinful activities under control and within the bounds of "moderation", are not sinners. Yet, the Bible tells us that if we have broken one of the laws we have broken them all. Can we not also use this truth to understand that sin is sin, regardless of our attempt to place degrees of sinfulness on things where God has not?

What are the pitfalls in our moderation excuse? Satan uses this, I believe, as one of his deadliest ploys to deceive and snare us. He opens a door into which we place one foot, and slowly he lures us all the way inside.

A magazine article told of a woman who was founder and president of a national organization promoting the drinking of alcohol in moderation. She was arrested following an auto accident for driving under the influence of alcohol (about twice the legal limit). She was also charged with the death of a person in the other car involved. After her conviction and sentencing to a prison term, this woman admitted the failure of moderation mentality.

In addition to the possibility, and even probability, that a "little sinning" could become a consuming sin, there is another consequence of our moderation excuse. When we begin to ignore, compartmentalize, or justify sin on any level or to any degree, we also begin to separate ourselves from the fellowship of a Holy God. We still have our salvation, but our communication with the Lord is hindered, because we are living in an unrepentant state. We do not know the closeness we desire as his child. Our spiritual growth is stagnated. We may justify our beliefs to ourselves and to others, but we cannot deceive our Heavenly Father.

Some may disagree at this point that these two situations apply to them. Some may still believe that certain activities are fine for Christians if done in moderation. Some people, after all, can gamble without becoming compulsive gamblers. Some may drink without becoming alcoholics. Some may be able to view pornography without it becoming all-consuming. Some may claim to live as good Christians and to have a fellowship with God that is "close enough".

So why should the moderation excuse not be used by the Christian disciple? The answer comes from Jesus himself. Listen to one of his sternest warnings to his followers:

> "And whoever welcomes a little child like this in my name welcomes me. But if anyone causes one of these little ones who believe in me to sin, it would be better for him to have a large millstone hung around his neck and to be drowned in the depths of the sea.
>
> "Woe to the world because of the things that cause people to sin! Such things must come, but woe to the man through whom they come!" (Matthew 18:5–7)

In other words, the follower of Christ must not be a stumbling block to others. Period! Jesus didn't allow any "wiggle room". He was firm—"WOE to the man (or woman) . . . !" We must not through our actions, no matter that it is in moderation, influence others in a way that leads to sin.

How many young people have justified their entry into gambling, drinking, or pornography because they witnessed a Christian involved in one of these? So often the young person watching, perhaps a son or daughter, will take to the extreme what a Christian may do in moderation. How many alcoholics, with a trail of broken homes behind them, wander the streets today because of one Christian who was a stumbling block?

What kind of witness do we choose to be? Do we want others to witness our "sins of moderation" and become mired in sin? Or do we want to give witness to the power of the blood of Jesus Christ to overcome sin? Is the cause of Christ great enough to lay down these sinful habits that stifle our fellowship and could prove deadly to others? Are we willing, for Christ, to be a living sacrifice—not in moderation but in the EXTREME?

YOUR TURN:

(1) Please read James 1:13–15, and Romans 14.
(2) Does "moderation mentality" lead you to progressively more temptations?
(3) What sin are you condoning in your life that you excuse with the "moderation excuse"?
(4) Do you want to be responsible for someone else living a life of alcoholism because of your drinking in moderation?
(5) Will you listen to the Holy Spirit's convicting voice regarding these "sins of moderation"?
(6) Pray that God will identify the moderation excuses in your life.

Part Eight

At His Feet

CHAPTER 16

WORTH IT

A woman came with an alabaster jar of very expensive perfume, made of pure nard. She broke the jar and poured the perfume on Jesus' head.

Some of those present were saying indignantly to one another, "Why this waste of perfume? It could have been sold for more than a years wages and the money given to the poor." And they rebuked her harshly.

Mark 14:3–5

About 20 years ago I was a store manager of a retail electronics chain. Once a year a coupon was placed in the store's sale flyer for a free flashlight. While a couple of employees and I were at the counter waiting on customers, an elderly lady walked into the store with a free flashlight coupon in her hand. One of the employees saw what she was holding, reached under the counter, and handed her a flashlight. Normally we would mention to the customer that batteries would be needed; but the employee was occupied with another customer, and the elderly lady walked quickly out of the store.

Out of a Distant Land

A few minutes later this same lady returned holding the flashlight and flipping the switch back and forth. She indignantly said, "This thing doesn't work!" The same employee who gave her the no-light flashlight calmly explained to her that it needed batteries to work and that they were not included. The lady slammed the free flashlight down on the counter and exclaimed, "Well then, **it's not worth it!**"

Much attention is given these days to what something is worth. If your interest is in antiques and collectibles, there are many appraisal shows on television and many books on the value of different items.

Much attention also is given to the worth of people and businesses. Magazines have an annual list of the 500 people and the 500 businesses that have the greatest worth. Of course, this "worth" is based on the value of the assets held by the person or business and is measured strictly in dollar terms.

We read the story in Mark 14 of a woman who had something of great worth that was kept in an alabaster jar. When she broke open the jar and poured it on the head of Jesus, those gathered around cried out, "Waste!"

How often today we hear the same cry when those with great assets, whether financial or personal, give what they have for the sake of Christ, and it is called "waste". Talented musicians sing and play in churches and other Christian gatherings rather than pursuing lucrative careers in other music venues. And the world calls it "waste".

Doctors and surgeons, who could be reaping handsome incomes in big-city practices and hospitals, instead become medical missionaries to third-world countries. Business leaders leave hard-won positions to start ministries. The world cries, "waste!"

Waste has been defined as giving something too much for something too little. Did this woman give something too much? Jesus answered that question with these words to those who cried, "Waste!"

> *"Leave her alone. Why are you bothering her? She has done a beautiful thing to me . . . She did what she could."*

What the world may call "waste", Jesus called "a beautiful thing". And this woman has been honored for all time for what she did.

Jesus is calling for us to break open our own alabaster jar, that which is most precious to us, and pour it out to him. Why? Because he alone is **worth it**! He alone is worth our time, our resources, our talents, our praise—he is worth the whole of our life.

We can never give something too much for him. When we realize the true worth of our Lord, no alabaster jar of our life will remain sealed . . . or unbroken.

YOUR TURN:

(1) What's in your alabaster jar? What is most valuable to you?

(2) Are you willing to "pour out" the most valuable thing you possess?
(3) Is Jesus worth being broken?
(4) What will remain when you are gone, the alabaster jar or the legacy of a sacrificial life?
(5) Pray that you will be broken and poured out.

CHAPTER 17

THE FIVE SENSES

"One thing I do know. I was blind but now I see!"
John 9:25

My wife, Jill, still laughs when she recalls a teachable moment she had with our son, Brett, when he was about four. She was putting him to bed one evening when Brett began the question game, "Mom, what would happen if we didn't have ears?"

Jill decided this would be a great time to give Brett a lesson on the five senses, "You tell me. What could you not do if you didn't have ears?"

"Hear!"

"Very good. What could you not do if you didn't have eyes?"

"See!"

"Right. What could you not do if you didn't have a mouth?"

"Eat!" (His definition of taste—food never stayed in his mouth long enough to taste).

"Now what could you not do if you didn't have a nose?"

This one he had to give some thought, but finally he figured it out.

"Pick boogers!"

You probably know the five senses: taste, smell, sight, touch, and hearing. We learned these early in life and usually think nothing of them in the course of the day. But imagine what would be different if we lacked or lost one of the senses?

Of the five senses, which would you least want to lose? Most people would probable say their sight. All senses serve a specific purpose, but sight seems to be the most critical for us to function and to enjoy the beauty around us.

Jesus healed many who lacked sight during his time on earth. One such healing is recorded in John. This particular man was blind from birth, and Jesus used his condition as a teachable moment for his disciples. He explained,

> "This happened so that the work of God might be displayed in his life." (John 9:3)

Jesus spit on the ground and made some mud, which he put on the man's eyes. He instructed him,

> "Go. Wash in the Pool of Siloam." So the man went and washed, and came home seeing. (John 9:7)

This incident caused quite a stir with this man's neighbors. They could not believe it was he. They wanted to know how his eyes were opened. The once-blind man explained what a man named Jesus had done.

The Pharisees entered the controversy. They began questioning him on his new sight. They didn't want to believe it was the same man who had once been blind. They called for his parents, and his parents confirmed that he was their son. They could not explain, though, how he received his sight.

Finally the Pharisees tried to condemn Jesus as a sinner who deserved none of the glory for what had occurred. To this the man replied,

> "Whether he is a sinner or not, I don't know. One thing I do know. I was blind but now I see!" (John 9:25)

When we are born again into the Kingdom of God, a remarkable, miraculous thing happens. We receive sight where before we were blind. There is light where before there was darkness. Jesus gives us that sight. Jesus is that light.

It is, of course, a spiritual sight leading us out of spiritual darkness. The truths of the spiritual realm suddenly come into focus, and we understand them as His truth.

The story of the once-blind man continues with the Pharisees hurling insults at him. His response reveals that the sight this man had received was more than physical sight:

> "Now that is remarkable! You don't know where he comes from, yet he opened my eyes. We know that God does not listen to sinners. He listens to the godly man who does his will. Nobody has ever heard of opening the eyes of a man born blind. If this man were not from God, he could do nothing."
>
> (John 9:30–33)

Jesus had indeed opened his eyes—physically as well as spiritually.

Jesus still heals those born blind. And while we may not know all the hows of our transformation, all who have known the Savior's touch can say, "One thing I do know. I was blind but now I see."

YOUR TURN:

(1) What "work of God" was displayed in this blind man's life?
(2) Please read John 9:4–5. Why do you suppose Jesus made the statement, "I am the light of the world", during this encounter with the man born blind?
(3) What is the significance of obedience as seen in verse 7?

(4) What spiritual light bulb has been turned on for you lately?
(5) Pray a prayer of gratitude that God healed your spiritual blindness.

CHAPTER 18

JUNK DRAWER

If we confess our sins, he is faithful and just and will forgive us our sins and purify us from all unrighteousness.
                                                                   1 John 1:9

Every home has one. It is usually found in a high traffic area of the home, either the kitchen or the den. Yet, it is hidden from the view of guests. It epitomizes the definition of secret clutter. It is the **junk drawer**!

At times the junk drawer is used as a way station for junk mail between the mailbox and the trash can. Or it may be used as an "out-of-sight, out-of-mind" file for bills that are coming due. Generally, however, it contains a menagerie of items from our culture. These are some of the items found in our family's junk drawer: out-of-ink pens, dead or suspect batteries, sprung paper clips, "important" receipts, old pagers, obsolete cell phones, tape measurers, needles and pins, cables for video games, cables for who-knows-what, extension cords, thread, string, electrical and phone adapters, staples, staple remover, photos, and pennies. Maybe you should plan your own junk drawer inventory as a fun family bonding experience on a rainy Sunday afternoon.

The junk drawer defies the physical laws of matter and space. Matter is warped and compressed. Space is mysteriously expanded within the fourteen-inch wide, eight-inch deep, and twenty-inch long drawer. No matter how much junk the drawer already contains, more can always be added by just a push or shove.

Our junk drawer is found in the kitchen. From outward appearance, all is clean, neat, and orderly. Open the third drawer down from the top in the cabinet to the left of the stove, however, and the previous perception is destroyed.

Frequently I ask for something missing and someone suggests, "Look in the junk drawer." If I'm fortunate enough to see the item, another junk drawer phenomenon takes over. The thread and cord inhabitants somehow unwind themselves and intertwine around the items in the drawer. The result is the "bunching" effect. A single item cannot be removed without pulling out another twenty or more items bound by the thread and cord.

When we follow the laws of human nature, we tend to compartmentalize our lives. We believe that by placing different aspects of our life into different compartments (drawers), we can separate them in such a way that one will not affect the other. In that way, if one of our compartments were filled with undesirable elements (junk), it would not affect the overall perception of orderliness and cleanliness. This is true of the Christian who chooses to cling to "junk" from the old nature.

As Christians, we tend to keep this junk drawer hidden from public view. Certainly we must keep it closed to other Christians, lest we be found not to be "good Christians". We may even give the items in our drawer such names as our "weaknesses", our "shortcomings", our "inadequacies", or our "failures". If we examine more closely, however, we may see that we are hiding old habits, attitudes, impurities, and duplicities that found a way station between the **old nature** and **the cross**. We cannot hide this junk, however, from a caring Father.

A Holy God will not allow us to maintain the "junk drawer of the spirit". He will not condone that which clutters our thinking, disrupts our prayers, hinders our Christian witness, and mars our testimony. The common thread, which intertwines these destructive items and bunches them to prevent easy removal, is **rebellion**. Need we be reminded that rebellion is sin? Also helping to entwine is **pride**. Together they lead to an entanglement that keeps us from effectively representing our Lord.

Removing an item or two from our "junk drawer" will not solve the problem (example: "Maybe if I quit smoking, that will appease God"). What we need is a radical cleaning—**a heaven orchestrated cleansing**! Jesus teaches that the cleansing must come from within:

> *"Woe to you, teachers of the law and Pharisees, you hypocrites! You clean the outside of the cup and dish, but inside they are full of greed and self-indulgence. Blind Pharisees!*

First clean the inside of the cup and dish, and then the outside also will be clean." (Matthew 23:25–26)

What we really need is to toss that "junk drawer of the spirit" to the foot of the Cross! There the cleansing blood of Christ breaks the entwinement of rebellion and pride, and we are set free from the law of our old nature. Paul states this well:

But I see another law at work in the members of my body, waging war against the law of my mind and making me a prisoner of the law of sin at work within my members. What a wretched man I am! Who will rescue me from this body of death? Thanks be to God—through Jesus Christ our Lord! (Romans 7:23–25)

Thanks be to God! Just as Jesus cleansed the temple (Mark 11:15–16), he cleanses us, the temple of the Holy Spirit.

Let us not live our lives with the over-shadowing guilt of a JUNK DRAWER OF THE SPIRIT. Let us believe what we have been promised in 1 John 1:9–

*If we confess our sins, he is faithful and just and will **forgive** us our sins and **purify** us from all unrighteousness.*

YOUR TURN:

(1) Please read Romans 7, and Hebrews 12:1–2.
(2) What is "hidden" in your "junk drawer of the spirit"?

(3) As you name them, would you put them at the Cross and accept Christ's cleansing power?
(4) Commit to leaving your junk drawer open before Him until all is removed.
(5) Pray for his radical cleansing power.

Part Nine

In His Steps

CHAPTER 19

RUN THE RACE

I do not run like a man running aimlessly.
1 Corinthians 9:26

Saint Paul must have been a runner. Many times in his writings he makes references to runners and to running the race. His running analogies are used in helping us to better understand the Christian life.

As a runner myself, I can identify with Paul. Just as Paul was running before the "jogging craze" of the 1970's, I, too, began running prior to that, in the 1960's. At that time it was considered a little strange. "Why are you running?" Someone would ask. "I'm not sure," would be my reply. Over three decades later, I'm still not sure. It's not a question a runner can necessarily answer.

My daughter, Meagan, became a runner in her early teenage years. Together we began running many of the 5K races near home and called each other "running bud". She won quite a few trophies for first and second place in her age group. Dad was proud. More important than her trophies, however, was the reminder she had written in ink across the top of her hand: 1 COR. 9:24–25. The passage is from the runner Paul:

> *Do you not know that in a race all the runners run, but only one gets the prize? Run in such a way as to get the prize. (Verse 24)*

Of course, there is a much deeper meaning in "get the prize" than simply the trophy given for winning a 5K race. Our Lord himself gives the prize to which Paul refers. The prize is worth our running.

Paul continues with the analogy:

> *Everyone who competes in the games goes into strict training. They do it to get a crown that will not last; but we do it to get a crown that will last forever. (Verse 25)*

The first part of this verse refers to the runners like those of us running the local road races. We train diligently, but our trophies are only temporary. An eternal crown, however, awaits the running disciple.

Many Christians will raise their hand in affirmation when asked, "Are you running the race?" A more relevant question would be, "Are you running God's race?"

Far too many, who call themselves Christians, are running the race of the world. "Rat race" is the most common term given to the world's race. It is a race revolving around an endless circle, a race having no lasting meaning, a race having no winners, and a race perpetually destroying the soul. Since it is a race with such lack of purpose, we should drop out—whatever the cost. Too many have spent a lifetime running the race, only to discover in the end that it had been the wrong race. We must be a runner in God's race. It is the only race worth running. Listen again to God's runner:

> *I consider my life worth nothing to me, if only I may finish the race and complete the task the Lord Jesus has given me—the task of testifying to the gospel of God's grace. (Acts 20:24)*

God's race is a testimony of God's grace and is worth the spending of our life to run. It is, further, the only race that gives our life meaning. This is expressed confidently by running brother, Paul:

> *I do not run like a man running aimlessly. (1 Corinthians 9:26)*

Stop now and examine your life. Can you say that you are running with purpose, or are you running the aimless race of the world that inevitably leads to defeat?

How, then, do we persevere and run God's race? The writer of Hebrews was also a runner, and through his words we are given the answer:

> *Let us run with perseverance the race marked out for us.* **Let us fix our eyes on Jesus,** *the author and perfecter of our faith, who for the joy set before him endured the cross, scorning its shame, and sat down at the right hand of the throne of God.* **Consider him** *who endured such opposition from sinful men, so that you* **will not grow weary and lose heart.** *(Hebrews 12:1–3)*

By fixing our eyes on Jesus and considering what he endured for the joy to come, we, also, will run and not grow weary and lose heart. And our words will be the same as those spoken to Timothy during Paul's final days, as he was being "poured out like a drink offering":

I have fought the good fight, I have finished the race, I have kept the faith. (2 Timothy 4:7)

YOUR TURN:

(1) Which race can you honestly claim to be running? The world's? God's?
(2) Think of the laboratory rat running on a treadmill. Despite all his efforts, running faster and faster, he gets nowhere. Do you consider all your efforts to be as meaningless also?
(3) Do you need to get off the treadmill?
(4) Will you commit to running God's race? Will you start today?
(5) Pray for true insight into which race you are now running.

CHAPTER 20

A MIRROR'S BEAUTY

And we, who with unveiled faces all reflect the Lord's glory, are being transformed into his likeness with ever-increasing glory, which comes from the Lord, and who is the Spirit.
2 Corinthians 3:1

People in business often share "customer stories" with one another. A man I know in the glass and mirror business related one of his stories to me.

A rather wealthy lady had wanted a large, elaborate mirror to go above a mantle in her house. This was no small mantle or small room or small house, so the mirror man created the worthiest mirror that he could. It was made of thick glass with wide beveled edges set in a gilded frame.

A couple of weeks after the mirror had been installed, a friend of the lady came by the mirror man's business and was practically begging him for exactly the same mirror to be placed above her mantle. She had been overcome by the beauty of the mirror at her friend's house and just had to have one, also. The same type mirror was made to fit the space above this lady's mantle, set in an identical frame, and installed.

A couple of weeks passed and this second lady came back to the mirror store. When she walked in the door the mirror man knew something was wrong. There was a look of despair all over the lady's face. She began voicing her displeasure, "My mirror is just not as beautiful as my friend's. I'm so disappointed."

The mirror man could have responded that she had an identical mirror to her friend's mirror, but in his wisdom he knew that wasn't the real problem. So he told her as diplomatically as he could, "A mirror doesn't have beauty in itself. A mirror only gets its beauty from what it reflects."

The beauty of our Christian life will not come **from whom we are**. It will come **from whom we reflect**.

When I was a freshman in college I joined the Baptist Student Union chapter on campus. A few weeks into the school year the BSU held a statewide convention for all the Georgia college chapters. We arrived at Rock Eagle campground near Eatonton on a Friday evening.

After getting off the buses we wandered around the camp trying to find our cabins. As I walked down the sidewalk I saw a college girl walking toward me. She looked very frail and stood no more than five feet tall. She leaned to one side and walked with a strange gait. One leg went one way and the other leg had to be pulled around beside it. Her arms were like twigs hanging by her side. Her front teeth protruded, and she wore very thick glasses.

My first inclination was to try to avoid her, but I could not. As we met she spoke a friendly "hello" accompanied by a broad smile. After she had passed I remember silently praying, "Thank you, God, for not making me like her."

The next night we all gathered in the auditorium for a worship service. As I took my seat I noticed that same misshapen girl sitting on the stage with three or four other college students. In my program I noticed a time allotted for personal testimonies, so I assumed that she was on stage for that purpose.

When the time came for her to give her testimony, she walked to the microphone with that awkward gait—and that broad smile covered her face. She began to share her experience as a Christian. She spoke of how blessed she was and how much joy was in her heart. She told of the peace and the purpose that God had given her. As she spoke, her very countenance filled the auditorium. **She reflected Christ!**

I bowed my head in shame when I recalled the prayer I had made the day before, "Thank you, God, for not making me like her." And I found myself praying instead, "O God, make me more like her."

She will always be in my memory. She had nothing in the world going for her, but she had everything that really mattered. **She was beautiful! She reflected Christ!**

YOUR TURN:

(1) Do you know someone whose Christian countenance fills the room?
(2) Can it not be so with each of us?
(3) When you look in the mirror make a habit of asking yourself, "Am I reflecting Christ?"
(4) Pray for a more Christ-like reflection.

CHAPTER 21

DEFINING MOMENT

He went away a second time and prayed, "My Father, if it is not possible for this cup to be taken away unless I drink it, may your will be done."

Matthew 26:42

He was said to have great potential as a quarterback for a college football team. Although only a sophomore, he had shown exceptional talent and confidence during the first two games of the season. Those games, however, had been "warm up" games for the season ahead and were against relatively weak opponents. The real test came in game three.

His team found itself behind by three touchdowns at halftime in that pivotal third game. But this unproven sophomore quarterback led his team to a come-from-behind victory in the second half with a brilliant display of passing, running, and error-free execution. One of the television sports announcers made the comment at the conclusion of the dramatic victory, "Today was truly a defining moment for this young quarterback."

"Defining moment" is a term we frequently hear, usually in the context of some well-known person. It is used in relation to a decision made or action taken at some pivotal point in a person's life. The response to a situation "defines" who the person is and will become.

Businesses, as well, have defining moments when strategic decisions are made that will define the success and viability of a company. The same may be said of nations. Consider the two centuries of our nation's history, and particular defining moments can be ascertained. The War Between the States, in fact, defined whether we would remain "The United States of America".

What pivotal points in Jesus' life could be described as "defining moments"? The case could be made for a number of such instances, from Satan's temptation to the nailing on the Cross. Let's look more closely at a particular point that, I believe, truly defines the life and mission of Christ.

After three years of ministry, Jesus knew the time was near to be betrayed into the hands of the enemy. He had preached to the multitudes, healed the sick outwardly and inwardly, taught those who would listen, and discipled his followers. But he had also raised the ire of the religious powers-that-be, and that would be his undoing.

When Jesus and his disciples had finished supper in the upper room, he led them to a place called Gethsemane. As he walked with Peter, James, and John, the Bible tells us that Jesus began to be "sorrowful and troubled". Then he said to them,

> *"My soul is overwhelmed with sorrow to the point of death."* (Matthew 26:38)

After all that Jesus had done in his ministry, one thing remained. The weight of it bore down upon Jesus as he sought a place to talk with the Father. The story continues:

> *Going a little farther, he fell with his face to the ground and prayed, "My Father, if it is possible, may this cup be taken from me."* (Matthew 26:39a)

This was the pivotal point for Jesus and his mission on earth. All that had happened to this point would be without context, if not for the next moment—**The defining moment.**

Even though he knew what was required to complete the mission, it was agony for his human body to imagine the suffering of the next few hours. Not only would it be the weight of his body as it pressed down on the nails through his hands and feet, but it would also be the weight of the sins of the world that caused Jesus such anguish.

> *And being in anguish, he prayed more earnestly, and his sweat was like drops of blood falling to the ground.* (Luke 22:44)

Three times Jesus fell on his face with the plea,

> *"Father, **if it is possible**, may this cup be taken from me."*

But it was not possible for the greatest mission in human history to be completed without Jesus' drinking from the cup before him.

"Yet not as I will, but as you will." (Matthew 26:39b)

In that statement of surrender we find the **defining moment**. The entire mission of Jesus on earth, Son of Man and Son of God, is defined in that one moment—**to do the will of the Father!**

Many times Jesus had told his disciples that he was on a mission from the Father. Yet, in the pivotal moment of Gethsemane, his mission was defined in its truest sense.

We have a mission as disciples of our Lord. When we seek that mission through his Word and his Spirit, he will lead us into our Garden of Gethsemane. We may also fall on our face in anguish, because we are asked to sacrifice. Rarely is it the sacrifice of death at the hands of others, but it is something equally painful. Our sacrifice is the surrender of our will to his will.

We plod through our Christian walk believing that somehow we can complete the mission without it, but there must be a **defining moment** in our Garden of Gethsemane when we pray the prayer of Jesus:

"NOT AS I WILL, BUT AS YOU WILL."

YOUR TURN:

(1) How would you define your Christian walk?
(2) What decisions or responses have contributed to that definition?

(3) Is there a decision or response that you need to make at this time, which will define your Christian commitment?
(4) Think of other pivotal points in Christ's mission. In your own mission.
(5) Have you had a Garden of Gethsemane?
(6) Pray sincerely for God's will to define your will.

CHAPTER 22

THEY OPENED THEIR EYES

Then he turned to his disciples and said privately, "Blessed are the eyes that see what you see. For I tell you that many prophets and kings wanted to see what you see but did not see it, and to hear what you hear but did not hear it."
Luke 10:23–24

The President of the United States liked to take an early morning jog. One particular morning he donned his shorts, tee shirt, and sneakers and began running down the sidewalk around the White House.

While he was running, he spotted a small boy with a box beside him sitting on the curb. The President signaled for his entourage of Secret Service men and reporters to stop.

"What's in the box?" The President asked the boy.

"Puppies," replied the boy.

"What kind of puppies are they, Whigs or Bull Moose?" Since the President was a Whig, he hoped to garner future votes for his party (obviously the political parties are changed here for the sake of harmony).

"They're Whig puppies, sir." the boy said with assurance.

"Great! That's great!" The President began to see how this encounter could be used for the greater good.

He hurriedly jogged back to the White House where the Vice-president was waiting. The VP was in the middle of a Presidential campaign to replace the President at the end of his tenure.

"Veep," the President exclaimed, "I've got a great photo-op for you!" He then explained his encounter with the boy and his puppies and suggested the VP go jogging the next day and take with him a number of reporters. What a great picture it would make for campaign brochures, and what a great story the "Whig puppies" would be for the evening news. The VP readily agreed in the wisdom of this opportunity.

The next morning Veep left in his jogging gear and headed down the sidewalk where the President had directed. In the group with him were plenty of reporters with cameras slung by their side.

The VP rounded a corner and just as he had hoped, the boy was sitting on the curb with the box beside him. Veep came to a halt, positioned himself by the boy and his box, made sure the reporters had their cameras ready, and began the script prepared for him.

"Hi, young man. What do you have in the box?"

"Puppies."

"Well, that's great. And what kind of puppies are they, Whigs or Bull Moose?" The cameras were clicking and videos were taping the VP's performance.

"They're Bull Moose puppies, sir."

"Bull Moose!" Veep was furious. "Why, I know for a fact that yesterday you told the President that the puppies were Whig puppies!"

"That's right, sir," the boy calmly explained, "but last night they opened their eyes."

What had those puppies experienced? They had experienced **a revelation!**

Throughout the accounts of Jesus with his first disciples we see the phrase, "the disciples did not understand". One such incident is recorded in Mark 9. Jesus said to his disciples:

> "The Son of Man is going to be betrayed into the hands of men. They will kill him, and after three days he will rise." But they did not understand what he meant and were afraid to ask him about it. (Mark 9:31–32)

Many parts of scripture we do not understand. Many happenings in our life we do not understand. Hard lessons are presented to us that we do not understand. Tragedies occur that we do not understand. Yet, if we are truly committed, fully devoted followers of Jesus Christ, we will experience what the early disciples experienced—**revelations**.

After Peter's declaration of Jesus' true identity, "You are the Christ, the Son of the living God," Jesus replied, "Blessed are you, Simon son of Jonah, for this was not revealed to you by man, but by my Father in heaven" (Matthew 16:16–17). Notice the source of Peter's revelation—**the Father in heaven**. That is the source of all our revelations concerning Jesus. That is our source of all the spiritual insights and all the revelations that contribute to our growth as Christian disciples. These divine revelations cannot come from man.

Jesus teaches us further in Matthew 11 that revelation comes not from position but from disposition:

> *"I praise you, Father, Lord of heaven and earth, because you have hidden these things from the wise and learned, and revealed them to little children."*
>
> Matthew 11:25

He speaks of the special insight enjoyed by the true disciple:

> *"For I tell you the truth, many prophets and righteous men longed to see what you see but did not see it, and to hear what you hear but did not hear it."*
>
> Matthew 13:16–17

During Jesus' final hours with his disciples he tells them of what lies ahead:

> *"But when he, the Spirit of truth, comes, he will guide you into all truth . . . He will bring glory to me by taking from what is mine and making it known to you . . . In a little while you will see me no more, and then after a little while you will see me."*

The disciples were confused:

They kept asking, "What does he mean by 'a little while'? We don't understand what he is saying."

Jesus continued:

"Ask and you will receive, and your joy will be complete." "Though I have been speaking figuratively, a time is coming when I will no longer use this kind of language but will tell you plainly about my Father. In that day you will ask in my name."

Then Jesus' disciples said,

"Now you are speaking clearly and without figures of speech. Now we can see that you know all things and that you do not even need to have anyone ask you questions. This makes us believe that you came from God"

Jesus answered,

"You believe at last!"
(John 16:13, 14, 16, 18, 24–26, 29–31)

Through the process of our spiritual development, God's Holy Spirit directs us into the truths of His Kingdom. When we come to Him as little children; when we seek him through His Word; when we live in daily communion with Him; He will open the eyes of our heart, and we will have revelations that only He can give us.

YOUR TURN:

(1) Do you ever consider why there is such a wide variance of beliefs concerning certain social issues? Why does each side adamantly believe their side is right?
(2) Do you understand why God's revelations are essential to doing his will and knowing him better?
(3) Are you watching for what God is ready to reveal concerning a particular aspect of your life? (Job, for example)
(4) How many times do you read a verse of scripture and receive different revelations from the same verse at different times?
(5) Pray that God will reveal his will in a particular financial step you are about to make.

Part Ten

Gone Fishing

CHAPTER 23

THE BIG ONE(S) THAT GOT AWAY

When he had finished speaking, he said to Simon, "Put out into deep water, and let down the nets for a catch." Simon answered, "Master, we've worked hard all night and haven't caught anything. But because you say so, I will let down the nets." When they had done so, they caught such a large number of fish that their nets began to break.

Luke 5:4–6

Someone asked me why I use so many fishing analogies. It's simple. Golf analogies are just not biblical. I know ministers and lay speakers often try to draw spiritual manna from a golf ball, but it's impossible to find a scriptural text that **directly** relates to the game of golf.

Furthermore, we should take note who Jesus chose as his first disciples—**fishermen** (I know the golfers are quoting Jesus at this point—"I have not come to call the righteous, but sinners to repentance"). It's also important to note that he immediately taught them how to catch a lot of fish (Luke 5:4–7). Had golf any spiritual purpose or significance, I'm sure it would have been introduced by first century disciples, not nineteenth century deacons.

Honestly, though, I chose the sport of fishing on remote streams for a sound reason—**failure is so much less public**. Hit a bad tee shot and people see it and snicker. Miss a three-foot putt and your "friends" roll their eyes. Failure is much more frequent in golf and much more visible.

The equivalent to missing a short putt in golf is having a "big one" get away in fishing. I've certainly had more than my share of lost trophies, but for the sake of brevity, I'll share only two experiences.

BIG ONE # 1

"In this world you shall have tribulation: but be of good cheer; I have overcome the world."
John 16:33(KJV)

When I was a boy of 10 or 11, my dad and I frequented a fishing hole in a dingy, deep creek meandering through the pasturelands. Usually we would catch a few bream and catfish, but would occasionally catch a bass.

During one of our summer afternoon trips, however, the "Hard Labor Creek Monster" rose to the surface, opened its large mouth as it rolled to take a hapless bug, and disappeared back to the murky depths. We began seeing this monstrous fish display itself on almost every trip. Its head and mouth looked like a bass, and we presumed it to be one of record proportions. Despite all our casting of various lures and baits, the behemoth proved wiser than we were.

Finally, toward the end of the summer, it happened. I hooked that fish of my youthful dreams! My screams of delight brought my Dad running to where I was on the bank. Playing the fish gently, I tried not to land him too quickly for fear of breaking the line, but a bush was in my way, and the line threatened to become entangled.

Dad took the rod from me and began walking around the bush, dragging the angry fish to the surface. It began thrashing and flopping and splashing as though a bomb were exploding. Then, suddenly, the commotion ceased, the rod flew back over my dad's head, and the limp line followed it into the air. The BIG ONE had broken the line and gotten away.

To say that I took that disappointing experience like a man would be far from accurate. I CRIED BIG TEARS! My heart was broken. The fish I had dreamed about all summer was momentarily at the end of my line, and I blamed my dad for letting him escape.

Dad tried to console me, saying something like, "It's not the end of the world . . . The sun will rise again in the morning, . . .". But it did no good. I cried big tears. Never would there be another fish like that one, and it had gotten away. Dad lost MY FISH!

If you think the analogy for this story relates to the importance and necessity of forgiveness, you're mistaken. It's only been about 37 years. I'll get around to forgiving my dad eventually.

The lesson I seek to convey from this story is the handling and overcoming of the inevitable disappointments we face in life. Crying big tears sometimes seems the only option, but since we are to have the Christian perspective, a more spiritually mature response should be adopted.

How do we perceive disappointments? Are disappointments seen as defeats? Do they often lead to despair? Do they rob us of our joy? Do we, who recognize the sovereignty of God, sometimes feel that maybe God made a mistake? When we view disappointments from a believer's perspective, we should realize that disappointments are necessary building blocks in our Christian character. Does that realization make disappointments any easier to accept? It certainly does not always. After all, disappointment is the product of failure to achieve or acquire something we very much desire.

All of us can name events or non-events that we would identify as disappointments. Varying degrees of disappointment are possible as well. Some disappointments leave us mildly bothered for a short time, while others may leave us devastated, requiring years to recoup.

How do we get beyond the disappointments that are bound to occur as long as we have breath? God is not silent about an occurrence so prevalent. Consider the following aspects of disappointment and God's instructions found in his Word.

Does our disappointment stem from the failure of an individual to meet our expectations? Perhaps that person is someone as close as our own child, who has fallen short of our desires for him or her. Nothing can break the heart of a parent more deeply. Or maybe our trust had been put in a friend or business partner, and they let us down. And how great is the disappointment when a spouse walks away from a marriage, and all the once-solemn vows are suddenly meaningless.

Great disappointment follows when we put our confidence in others, and they do not satisfy our expectations. When we put our trust in God rather than man, however, he will never disappoint. God is able and willing to go far beyond our expectations, as witnessed in his Word:

Now to him who is able to do immeasurably more than all we ask or imagine, according to his power that is at work within us . . . (Ephesians 3:20)

People will constantly fail us and cause us grief. God will sustain us. Listen to the Psalmist:

Those who know your name will trust in you, for you, Lord, have never forsaken those who seek you. (Psalms 9:10)

Hear also God's Word from Jeremiah:

This is what the Lord says: "Cursed is the one who trusts in man, who depends on flesh for his strength and whose heart turns away from the Lord . . . But blessed is the man who trusts in the Lord, whose confidence is in him. (Jeremiah 17:5, 7)

In addition, an examination of our attitude should be made when confronted with disappointments. After all, attitude most directly determines our response. We have the tendency to write off disappointments as complete failures, instead of looking for the opportunities they provide. Such was not the case with the prisoner Paul. Being confined to prison would be, for most of us, a very real failure. Notice, in contrast, Paul's attitude:

> *Now I want you to know, brothers, that what has happened to me has really served to advance the gospel. As a result, it has become clear throughout the whole palace guard and to everyone else that I am in chains for Christ. Because of my chains, most of the brothers in the Lord have been encouraged to speak the word of God more courageously and fearlessly. (Philippians 1:12–14)*

What for most of us would be extreme disappointment, Paul embraced with rejoicing. Can we, by taking an eternal perspective, not turn our disappointments into opportunities to further the gospel of Christ? What better way to reflect our trust in the Lord than to persevere in the face of personal disappointment.

Probably the cause of most of our disappointments emanates from leaving God out of our plans. How I could write a book on that subject alone! Whether in our home, our business, or our relationships, we so often make our plans and just expect God to sprinkle blessings as we go along. We believe that since we call ourselves by Christ's name, we are capable of making our plans outside of God's leading. And we are surprised when our plans don't go as we had hoped?

These are the words of Jesus' brother James:

Now listen, you who say, "Today or tomorrow we will go to this or that city, spend a year there, carry on business and make money." Why, you do not even know what will happen tomorrow . . . Instead, you ought to say, "If it is the Lord's will, we will live and do this or that." (James 4:13–15)

Disappointments will come to us all. It is a fact of life. It is inevitable. Many of our expectations will not be met. We will experience failures and broken dreams. Things will not happen as we had planned. How, then, do we find peace in the midst of disappointment as a child of God?

One verse, which most of us can recite by memory, holds the key to knowing that peace:

And we know that in all things God works for the good of those who love him, who have been called according to his purpose. (Romans 8:28)

We can recite the verse, but do we really believe it? When we practice the latter part of the verse, we will know the truth of the former. If we love God and place him above all else and are following in his purpose, then we will know that God uses every circumstance of life—even all our deepest disappointments—for our good.

Undoubtedly, the most deeply disappointed men in history were the eleven disciples as they watched the one, for whom they had forsaken all, being nailed to a cross. All was changed on the THIRD DAY!

By walking in complete submission and obedience to our Lord, our disappointments will also know their THIRD DAY.

YOUR TURN:

(1) What is the source of your greatest disappointments at this time?
(2) What are the Christian opportunities that these disappointments offer?
(3) Will you commit to seizing these opportunities?
(4) Are you making your plans without seeking Him in guiding your steps?
(5) Please read Jeremiah 17:5–8.
(6) Pray that God will show you his purpose in your latest disappointment.

BIG ONE #2

Jesus replied, "I tell you the truth, everyone who sins is a slave to sin."

John 8:24

My friend, Scott, had been asking me to go with him to his uncle's cabin located a few yards from a trout stream. Just as my teenage son never turns down food, I never turn down a trout fishing opportunity.

We were on the stream at the break of dawn and began catching a few average-sized rainbows. Towards the middle of the day we both waded into a pool about fifty feet across. The current cut into the opposite bank and made a gentle counter-clockwise eddy back towards us.

Casting an olive bead-head wooly booger upstream, I let it drift into the current. As it settled out of the current into the eddy water, I felt the familiar short tug. When I lifted my rod to set the hook, I knew a trophy had fallen victim to my favorite fly. The big fish immediately ran upstream to the head of the pool as I gave him line. As I turned him back toward the pool he surfaced for the first time, and I saw him to be a whopping brown trout in the 24–26 inch range. That's a nice trout for a small Georgia stream.

The fight continued as Mr. Brown swam to the depths of the pool. I eased him back toward the surface, and he surged downstream taking line as he went. Finally, he seemed to be tiring, and I began bringing him towards Scott. He had been watching the show intently and was standing out in the pool a few yards downstream from me. When the big trout was about six feet in front of Scott, I brought him to the surface, and Scott had his first good look at MY trophy.

"Gar', that one's going in the freezer!" Scott yelled.

Suddenly the fish found a second wind (I'm sure terrified by Scott's exclamation), reared back its head, rolled its broad body, and lunged in the opposite direction with all its strength. The bead-head wooly booger flew through the air and over my shoulder.

The surface of the water, the scene of a great battle just a moment earlier, calmed. Scott turned and looked at me, mouth wide open. I stood in shock, mouth clinched tight. With all the restraint I could muster, I gave Scott instructions for the future, "Scott, don't you EVER mention the freezer again until the trout is firmly in my grasp!"

Of course, it wasn't Scott's fault (but if it were, I've learned to forgive), and we both laughed. But it was disappointing.

Scott, ever the optimist, saw opportunity in this disappointing experience. He was in the Sunday school department where I served as director. Each Sunday morning I would give a devotional during assembly time.

"Gar', I just know there's a devotional in what just happened," Scott suggested.

Gone Fishing

There is, indeed, a devotional and a lesson to be learned. While most of us wouldn't want to be compared to a fish, allow me that liberty in this case.

Satan uses lures to entice us into his camp. Just as one lure will not work for every fish or on every day or in every circumstance, Satan uses different lures according to our weaknesses. He is cleaver, cunning, and deceitful. His lure is so irresistible as he dangles it in front of us. How could it possibly do us any harm? We go for it, but there's an unanticipated problem. **We don't see the hook.**

What are your weaknesses? Can you identify with any of these:

- Consuming desire for more material possessions
- Jealousies
- Lust of the eyes
- Impure thoughts
- Alcohol or other drugs
- Flirtatiousness
- Greed
- Gossip
- _____

Just fill in the blank. Whatever our weakness, Satan has a lure that will be cast in our direction. Too often we fall for it. We see no harm in a little tasty morsel. However, there's one problem—THE HOOK!

Sin hooks us, and Satan tries to bring us over to his side. The big brown trout in the story threw the hook solely with his efforts. Ours is a different dilemma. Many times we realize what has happened, but it is too late. The hook is set past the barb. And, try as we might, with self-help books, seminars, and counselors, we just cannot shake it out.

How, then, is the hook removed? Like everything else in our Christian experience, it is not as we would naturally think. We must cease our own efforts to fight Satan's pull and give up. Please don't misunderstand, certainly we do not surrender to Satan, but we admit our total helplessness to remove the hook ourselves. Jesus died for this dilemma. It is his death that frees us from the barb of sin. We fall in our helplessness before the Cross in recognition of what has already been done and know that he alone can set us free.

Imagine what "the big one that got away" felt as the hook dislodged, and he again settled into the depths of the pool he called home. In a word—**Freedom**.

The good news is this: We do not have to be held captive to sin. Whatever it is that has us hooked today can die on the cross, and we can know the freedom of Christ and the indwelling fellowship of the Father.

> *Jesus replied, "I tell you the truth, everyone who sins is a slave to sin. Now a slave has no permanent place in the family, but a son belongs to it forever. So if the Son sets you free, you will be free indeed."* (John 8:34–36)

I can testify–**His word is truth**.

YOUR TURN:

(1) What are your weaknesses? List them.
(2) What kind of lures is Satan using to entice you?
(3) Does Satan presently have you hooked in a certain weakness?
(4) Recognize that Christ has already paid the price for your freedom.
(5) Please read Galatians 5:1.
(6) Pray in true repentance that God will grant you freedom from whatever has you hooked.

CHAPTER 24

NOT JUST A FLY ROD

Simon Peter answered, "You are the Christ, the Son of the living God."

Matthew 16:16

You may look at it and consider it just a worthless old fishing rod. You may not even understand how it was to be used. As fishing rods go, it's not much to look at.

It is a dirty burgundy in color and made of fiberglass. It measures nine feet from its reel seat to the slender tip. It is rather large by today's fly rod standards, probably a "9-weight", which would make it somewhat unwieldy on a small mountain stream. The cork handle has several small plugs missing, knocked out by falls and tree limbs. The reel is black enamel and chrome with much of the paint worn off around the edges. The plastic reel handle is bent, again probably the result of a fall. In the middle of the rod is a repair made by my dad. The rod was broken when a non-fishing mechanic threw a tire in the trunk of the car on top of the rod.

The rod bears the name of Ted Williams, who endorsed many fishing and sporting goods products for Sears. I remember saving paper route money for the rod and going with my parents to Sears to make my much-anticipated purchase. It was my first fly rod.

Looking at the rod now, you would think it to have little value. The repaired section causes it to have poor casting action. It is certainly no match for the light, wispy rods made today of hi-tech materials. But the memories associated with that rod could fill many pages. I remember casting a popping bug to surface-feeding bream as the sun gave way to the first stars. Dad was beside me cheering me on with each double-hand sized bream brought to the bank. I remember taking the rod on a mountain vacation and catching my first fly rod trout.

You cannot buy that rod from me. I would not trade it for a brand new top-of-the-line Orvis 5-weight fly rod. It has too much value to me. It's not just an old, battered rod—**It's my first fly rod.**

―――――

The question has circulated for 2000 years. Who was Jesus Christ? In the days that Jesus walked the earth the question arose constantly. Who was this man? Many believed they had the answer. The Pharisees asked the man born blind, who Jesus made to see, who is this man that healed you?

We know this man is a sinner. (John 9:24)

Gone Fishing

Nicodemus approached Jesus and said,

> *Rabbi, we know you are a **teacher** who has come from God. For no one could perform the miraculous signs you are doing if God were not with him. (John 3:2)*

The Samaritan woman at the well said to Jesus,

> *Sir, I can see that you are a **prophet**. (John 4:19)*

Jesus attended the Feast of Tabernacles and some of the people of Jerusalem began to ask,

> *Isn't this **the man they are trying to kill**? . . . Have the authorities really concluded that he is the Christ? (John 7:25–26)*

Some of the Jews even proclaimed,

> *We now know that you are **demon possessed**! (John 8:52)*

Later they picked up stones to stone him,

> *for blasphemy, because you, **a mere man**, claim to be God. (John 10:33)*

Jesus caused quite a stir among the religious leaders and others of that time. The result was much speculation—Who was he? Was he a mere man?

One account, which is perhaps most telling, involves Jesus' own questioning of his disciples.

> *When Jesus came to the region of Caesarea Philippi, he asked his disciples, "Who do people say the Son of Man is?"*

*They replied, "Some say **John the Baptist**; others say **Elijah**; and still others, **Jeremiah** or **one of the prophets**."*
"But what about you?" he asked. "Who do you say I am?"
*Simon Peter answered, "You are **the Christ, the Son of the living God**." (Matthew 16:13–16)*

Here we can discern the world's view of Christ during his life on earth, a view that varies still. Magazine articles, movies, television documentaries, and religious scholars all ask, WHO WAS JESUS?

Jesus asked, "Who do you say I am?" I AM. The more accurate question, therefore, would be, WHO IS JESUS? Our very salvation depends on our answer.

If you confess with your mouth, "Jesus is Lord," and believe in your heart that God raised him from the dead, you will be saved. (Romans 10:9)

Jesus asked, "But what about you?" What about us today as his disciples? Can we answer with the certainty of Simon Peter? And if we can, what does that declaration imply?

The old broken fly rod has no value to anyone else. But it has great value to me, because it's not just a rod, it's my first fly rod.

When we realize and confirm in our heart who Jesus was and who Jesus is, he will have value as nothing else in our lives. We will see the scars from his wounds and know that he was broken for us. We will trade him for nothing the world can offer. Because he's not just a man, HE IS THE CHRIST, THE SON OF THE LIVING GOD.

YOUR TURN:

(1) How firm is your conviction when asked, "Who is Jesus?"
(2) Is your answer based on reason or faith?
(3) Why is there still so much speculation about the identity of Jesus? (Please read Matthew 16:17–19 to help your understanding)
(4) Is settling the identity issue essential to discipleship?
(5) Pray for a more real fellowship with Jesus, the Son of God.

CHAPTER 25

THE ALWAYS POOL

Whoever drinks the water I give him will never thirst.
John 4:14

Certain places have special meaning. There's a place on a stream in the northeast corner of Georgia that holds special meaning for me. It's a place my Dad and I discovered over twenty years ago.

About 1980 we began fishing in a stream winding through the Blue Ridge foothills and managed to catch a few trout. It became a regular trip for us, and each time we went we would hike up the stream a little farther. One particular day the trout were not cooperating at all. We'd caught one or two and kept plodding up the stream in hopes our fish fortune would change.

Late in the afternoon we approached a section where the stream seemed to disappear behind and above some large boulders. When we climbed over those boulders, we found ourselves viewing the most beautiful sight anywhere on the stream. Water cascaded down a series of drops, falling thirty-five or forty feet into the pool below. The pool itself was contained within rock walls on both banks. One of the walls on the left was low enough for the water to fall over and into the pool.

After we had taken time to absorb the beauty of the scene, we began to cast, and immediately the fish cooperated. We were catching trout with almost every cast. The light of day was fading fast by then, but as we left we determined that pool would be our ultimate destination with each trip to the stream.

Over the last twenty years I have fished that stream countless times with my Dad and friends. My son caught his first trout on that stream, and we have held hundreds of trout from "the pool". My two daughters have also recently been admitted into this exclusive trout sanctuary.

But it was a regular fishing buddy of mine, Keith, who gave that special place its name—**the always pool**. It earned that name by **always** producing trout from its waters. No matter if we'd gone fishless all day, **the always pool** would **always** give us a trout to hold.

Not much warrants the term "always." We've come to believe that there are no guarantees or promises that will always hold true. Some products, services, or businesses may satisfy us for years. But at some point they let us down, and we resign ourselves to the belief that nothing is lasting or permanent.

Some people disappoint us as well. They pledge that they will always be there for us, but friendships dissolve when "always" doesn't mean always. Marriages end in divorce because "always" didn't really mean always.

Even the always pool, as much as I hesitate to admit, has failed to yield a trout on two or three occasions over the last two decades (it's still a special place).

Gladly I can testify, however, there is another ALWAYS POOL where ALWAYS means ALWAYS. From it flow waters that quench the deepest thirsts of the human heart. These are the waters of which Jesus spoke to the Samaritan woman at the well:

> "Everyone who drinks this water will be thirsty again, but whoever drinks the water I give him will never thirst. Indeed, the water I give him will become in him a spring of water welling up to eternal life." (John 4:13–14)

And if we "never thirst" then we will ALWAYS find water for the soul.

There is also the ALWAYS of his presence. Read again the last words of Jesus to his first disciples. In a world of the temporary and uncertain, we can find permanence and assurance in his promise:

> "I am with you ALWAYS, to the very end of the age." (Matthew 28:20)

YOUR TURN:

(1) Other than God's Word, does anything always hold true?
(2) Why, then, do we place such faith in the things that are bound to disappoint?
(3) Write down some promises of God that you have found always to hold true in your personal experiences.
(4) Pray with the certainty that he is always there.

Part Eleven

His Amazing Ways

CHAPTER 26

GOD WORKS

Great are the works of the Lord; they are pondered by all who delight in them.

Psalms 111:2

Billy Graham was asked by Larry King to give a one-sentence summation of his theology. Without hesitation Rev. Graham responded, "What a friend we have in Jesus!"

AMEN! It is such a simple answer, so to the point and so true.

How would we respond to such a question? How would we express our theology in a nutshell? Although I am certainly no theologian, I have considered the question and would respond according to my simple belief—GOD WORKS!

Throughout God's word it is evidenced. Throughout our life it is manifested. GOD WORKS!

The beginning of that revelation is recorded in the first verse of Genesis.

In the beginning God created the heavens and the earth. And the entire Old Testament is the story of God working in the lives of his children.

The record of God's work continues into the New Testament with the sending of his only Son. Here we see God's redemptive work, a work that will forever span the chasm between man and God.

The earliest record of Jesus' life portrays a boy already busy doing his Father's work. As we walk with him through the Gospel accounts, we are shown a Savior who worked among the people of his day. With his touch the blind were made to see, and with his voice the lame were made to walk. He took away the sores of the lepers and cleansed from without. More importantly, he took away sin and cleansed from within. He identified hypocrisy and revealed the Father's truth.

Jesus' healing of an invalid man is told in the fifth chapter of John. The Jews were incensed that his healing had been done on the Sabbath and began persecuting Jesus. *Jesus said to them, "My Father is always at his **work** to this very day, and I, too, am **working**"* (John 5:17). How revealing are those words of Christ. Yet, the religious people of the day were blind to God's working and were only concerned with the letter of the law.

In the last few solemn hours Jesus spent with his disciples before he would be crucified, the meaning behind God's work within the disciples' lives was explained. Jesus used an illustration that would be easily understood, and he portrayed his Father as the chief worker. *"I am the true vine, and my Father is the gardener"* (John 15:1). The purpose of God's work in this illustration is simple. He works as the gardener so that we as Christ's disciples will bear much fruit. As a branch of the True Vine, we are lifted up and pruned so that we will be the bearer of the fruit produced through him.

Jesus promised his disciples that when he was no longer with them, he would send the Holy Spirit to work in the lives of believers to expose the guilt of the world:

> *"When he comes, he will convict the world of guilt in regard to sin and righteousness and judgment . . . When he, the Spirit of truth, comes, he will **guide you** into all truth."* (John 16:8, 13)

As we study the Scriptures we realize that God's active, working relationship with his children is an integral part of his character. We will also realize that the same working relationship applies to our individual circumstances. God is at work in our daily lives. His work is not just past history. The creation of the earth and sky was a magnificent work, but his crowning achievement was the creation of man—in his image, for a relationship, for a fellowship, for a purpose, for his work on earth.

> *For we are God's **workmanship**, created in Christ Jesus to do **good works**, which God prepared in advance for us to do. (Ephesians 2:10)*

We are his workmanship and at the same time, we are his workers. A special relationship of MASTER and AP-

PRENTICE comes to mind. We as his apprentice are to do the good works that the Master has prepared for us to do.

What is required in being God's apprentice? Consider the following responsibilities to him, and his promises to us:

- LEARN THE WORK OF THE MASTER. He has worked to save us, to draw us into a saving knowledge of Jesus Christ, and to put us into a working relationship as his apprentice. The best way to learn his work is to KNOW HIM. We learn to know him through the disciplines of prayer, meditation, study of his Word, and walking in faith and trust. We heed Christ's call to follow, and when we follow we know him more intimately as he works through us. The Master's works are good works, which he prepared in advance for us to do.

- DISCOVER OUR OWN SPIRITUAL GIFTS through the work of the Holy Spirit. His Spirit will "guide us into all truth" concerning our gifts. Once we know the gifts with which the Master blesses us, then we can more effectively use those gifts for his purpose. God uses us differently according to our different abilities and gifts, but we must remember the source of authority for the work.

  > *There are different kinds of **working**, but the same God **works** all of them in all men. (1 Corinthians 12:6)*

- AS APPRENTICES, WE GO TO WORK. One of the most daunting tasks we have as a Christian apprentice is found in Philippians 2:12.

> *Continue to **work out** your salvation with fear and trembling . . .*

For so many years I did not understand that verse. Somehow I believed that accepting Christ as Savior immediately put me on a spiritual autopilot. We must, however, "WORK OUT" our salvation by making the choices that are in harmony with God's will. In other words, we must practice obedience.

> *. . . for it is God who **works** in you to will and to act according to his good purpose.* (Philippians 2:13)

The master works to conform our will to his, so that our actions will reflect his purpose.

- AS A WISE MASTER WORKMAN, GOD DOESN'T PUT US TO WORK WITHOUT PROPER TOOLS. He equips us to do his work. A church marquis recently caught my attention with these words: "God doesn't call the qualified, he qualifies the called." We may believe we will be qualified and equipped as soon as we are ready to go to work. That is often not the case, however. Many times God equips us for work over a long period of time. We sometimes will not even be aware of this equipping until the time arrives to go to work. Then we will understand the way in which God worked to provide the tools we would need for a particular assignment.

> *May the God of peace . . . **equip** you with everything good for doing his will, and may he*

work in us what is pleasing to him, through Jesus Christ. (Hebrews 13:20–21)

- **THE MASTER KNOWS THAT THE APPRENTICE WILL SOMETIMES GROW WEARY AND EXPERIENCE DISCOURAGEMENT.** He will provide the means to persevere. Imagine the ordeals of the Apostle Paul during his missionary journeys. His is a study in "what can possibly go wrong next". Yet, God sustained him in his mission work, and Paul persevered and completed the work. Take note of three instances when the Master intervened in Paul's work to provide the means to persevere:

    > *To this end I labor, struggling with all **his energy**, which so powerfully **works** in me. (Colossians 1:29)*

    > *I can do everything **through him who gives me strength**. (Philippians 4:13)*
    > ***His power** is at **work** within us. (Ephesians 3:20)*

- **THE MASTER ENSURES AND PROMISES THAT OUR WORK FOR HIM IS NOT IN VAIN.** The world glorifies the work of man, but the work of man crumbles with time and will eventually fall in ruins. The Master's work through us endures for all time. We may never see the end product of our labor in this world, but I believe we will know it when God reveals it to us in the world to come. Let us work, then, with all our might.

    > *Therefore, my dear brothers, stand firm. Let nothing move you. Always give yourselves fully*

*to the **work** of the Lord, because you know that your labor in the Lord **is not in vain**. (1 Corinthians 15:58)*

GOD WORKS—in me, through me, for me—FOR HIS PURPOSE. In no way can I reflect upon my life and come to any other conclusion—GOD WORKS. Together as Master and apprentice we are "CO-LABORERS" in the Kingdom of God. To think that he loves me enough to make me a vital part of his work here on earth, and to think that a reward awaits me to continue his work—not bound by earthly constraints, but as one with the Master—I can only respond in humility.

WHAT A PRIVILEGE! WHAT GRACE!

YOUR TURN:

(1) What is your theology "in a nutshell"?
(2) Think of the ways God has worked in your life already.
(3) How is God working through you at this time?
(4) What is your view of heaven? Will we be put to work?
(5) Pray that God will show you the work he has for you and give you the strength to do it.

CHAPTER 27

GOD DOESN'T ADD

But the one who received the seed that fell on good soil is the man who hears the word and understands it. He produces a crop, yielding a hundred, sixty, or thirty times what was sown.

Matthew 13:23

A psychologist was having lunch with three friends of other professions. One was a mathematician, one a scientist, and the other a lawyer. The psychologist, always interested in observing various human responses, posed the same question to each of the three men.

He began with the mathematician, "What is two plus two?"

The mathematician quickly answered, "The sum would be four."

Turning to the scientist, the psychologist again posed the question, "What is two plus two?"

The scientist wrinkled his forehead in thought, "There are probably quite a few theories related to your question. I must meet with my colleagues, and we will begin experiments to determine the most plausible scientific explanation for each theory uncovered. After a second or third review of the data, we should have a reasonably confident answer for you. Give me a couple of years."

The responses given by the first two men had been exactly as the psychologist had anticipated. The lawyer, however, was the wildcard. "What is two plus two?" The lawyer was asked.

Leaning over the table with one hand cupped beside his mouth, the lawyer replied in a whisper, "What would you like for it to be?"

Since lawyers bear the brunt of a disproportional number of jokes, a lawyer friend assured me that this story has the BAR Association's stamp of approval.

With most everything in the realm of God's Kingdom, simple equations do not add up to the answer that we might rationally conclude. Let's consider a couple of examples.

My wife and I were married (1 + 1), and the resulting union now equals a family of five (1 + 1 = 5). Do the same math with your marriage. The equations will differ greatly (1 + 1 = 3, 1 + 1 = 12, 1 + 1 = 6, . . .). The math doesn't add up the same way we learned in school.

A seed, let's say a kernel of corn, is planted in the ground. The seed sprouts from the ground and produces a stalk upon which grow ten ears of corn, each of which has hundreds of kernels of corn. One seed alone equals thousands of seeds in this equation.

When we consider that only God is in control of both of these situations, one conclusion can be reached: GOD DOESN'T ADD! Am I saying that there is actually something that the God of the universe cannot accomplish? Am I saying that he is a limited God? On the contrary, I am saying that, in his greatness, he does not have use for simple addition. He will only MULTIPLY. When God is involved in a situation, the laws of addition just do not apply. God only multiplies.

We are each one seed, but God does not intend for us to remain an entity unto ourselves. He intends for our life to know his multiplying effect. The word the Bible often uses for this divine concept is **abound**. God wants himself to abound in us. He desires for us to abound in him. Read from God's Word of this truth:

> *And God is able to make all grace **abound** to you, so that in all things at all times, having all that you need, you will abound in every good work. (2 Corinthians 9:8)*

The product of this abounding grace is an abundant life in Christ:

> *"I am come that they might have life, and that they might have it more **abundantly**." (John 10:10[KJV])*

We are each one seed. How do we know God's multiplying effect in our life? Again it is impossible to determine by rational means. To live a life that is productive far beyond our own individual efforts, we must first, as does a seed, DIE. The seed must die before it can produce a harvest many times greater than itself. To know God's abounding grace, we must die to self and let him multiply our gift of self.

No verse of scripture expresses this truth more clearly than these words of Christ:

> "I tell you the truth, unless a kernel of wheat falls to the ground and dies, it remains only a single seed. But if it dies, it produces many seeds. The man who loves his life will lose it, while the man who hates his life in this world will keep it for eternal life. Whoever serves me must follow me; and where I am, my servant also will be. My Father will honor the one who serves me." (John 12:24–26)

DENY SELF—FOLLOW CHRIST—KNOW THAT GOD ONLY MULTIPLIES

YOUR TURN:

(1) Please read Matthew 13:11–13, and Matthew 25:28–30.
(2) Is God's abounding grace for your benefit alone?
(3) Look for evidence of God's multiplying effect in your life.
(4) Are you noticing that God works in irrational ways?

(5) Is your life producing a harvest? Have you died to self?
(6) Pray that you will be a conduit for his abounding grace.

CHAPTER 28

ONE MORE TIME, DADDY

For what I do is not the good I want to do; no, the evil I do not want to do—this I keep on doing.
                                                          Romans 7:19

When our youngest child Kellie was a preschooler she chose a form of recreation each evening that allowed for my participation. Coming home from work I would automatically sit in "my" easy chair, and she would automatically run up in front of me and stand with her hands out. I would pull her onto my knees and start bouncing them up and down in the time with the melody, "Ride the little horsey up to town, watch out, Kellie, don't fall down!" And with the "down" I would straighten my legs, and she would slide down to the floor in a heap.

Jumping up from the floor she would hop back on my knees with the plea, "One more time, Daddy!" Five falls later she would again hop up on my knees with the same impossible-to-resist plea, "One more time, Daddy, just one more time!" This would continue until my wife would save me with the call for dinner, and our game would end.

Someone once said to me, "My sins are mostly reruns." That's a very true observation. Our sins do seem to be mostly "reruns". Why is it that we are plagued by the same weaknesses and sin? How often we have to go before our heavenly Father and plead, "One more time, Father, just one more time, forgive me." We think we have kicked a sinful habit, but a short time later we fall again and have to come back in humility—"One more time, Father."

One of the most meaningful passages in the Bible to me is found in Romans 7. Paul addresses this dilemma of the sinful nature. He honestly confesses,

"I do not understand what I do. For what I want to do I do not do, but what I hate, I do . . . What a wretched man I am!" (Romans 7:15, 24)

We have such good intentions. We want to be good Christians. We do not want to sin. Yet, we find ourselves in our weakness falling to the same temptations. How can he forgive us "one more time"?

We can only know the scope of God's forgiveness when we look to **the Cross**. Jesus came "for the forgiveness of sin". His blood covers "all our sins". He "bore the sins of us all". Therefore, it is at the Cross where we can lay down our sins and find forgiveness by what Christ has already done. Paul does not end Romans 7 as a "wretched man".

He finishes with a praise, "Thanks be to God—through Jesus Christ our Lord." Paul knew the forgiveness of the Cross had already been accomplished.

Something amazing happens as we live a life of repentance. Something amazing happens as we know his forgiveness all those "one more times". His power works in us, and we learn to avoid those temptations of the sins that entangle us (those "besetting" sins). And we learn to love more and more a Father whose love never ignores our pleas of "one more time".

Jesus teaches us this in Luke 7. A Pharisee invited Jesus to dinner at his house. A woman who had lived a sinful life learned of Jesus' presence.

> *She brought an alabaster jar of perfume, and as she stood behind him weeping, she began to wet his feet with her tears. Then she wiped them with her hair, kissed them and poured perfume on them.*

The Pharisee was shocked. Didn't Jesus realize that this woman was a sinner? Jesus then gave this illustration:

> *"Two men owed money to a certain moneylender. One owed him five hundred denarii, and the other fifty. Neither of them had the money to pay him back, so he canceled the debts of both. Now which of them will love him more?"*

The answer is obvious. Jesus concluded the lesson:

> *"Therefore, I tell you, her many sins have been forgiven—for she loved much. But he **who has been forgiven little, loves little.**"*

I do not believe Jesus was saying that we should try to sin much. I do believe that he was emphasizing that this woman had known forgiveness of much sin and, therefore, had loved much. To know forgiveness we must live a life of repentance. Then we will know the scope of his forgiveness, and the overwhelming love of the Father. And we will love him more and more.

He answers our plea, "one more time", EVERY TIME.

YOUR TURN:

(1) Please read Romans 6:1–4. How does this relate to Romans 7?
(2) If we are dead to sin, why do we keep on sinning?
(3) Have you known the forgiveness of "much" sin? How does this affect your devotion to a merciful Father?
(4) Pray seeking forgiveness. Pray in true repentance and know he forgives.

CHAPTER 29

I WISH I WAS GOD

Once, having been asked by the Pharisees when the Kingdom of God would come, Jesus replied, "The Kingdom of God does not come with your careful observation, nor will people say, 'Here it is,' or 'There it is,' because the Kingdom of God is within you."

Luke 17:20–21

Boys just need super-heroes. Although I do not remember them called super-heroes when I was a boy, they were my heroes, and they were super.

My own personal favorite was Superman—not the phony, pseudo-Superman wannabees of the last ten or fifteen years. This was the real Superman, and I wanted to be like him.

With a red marker I would create the large "S" on a shirt. Safety pins would attach a towel to the shirt as a cape. Socks would be pulled up over my pants to imitate boots. In my mind I was Superman, and I could do all the heroic, super-human acts of Superman.

My son, Brett, followed in my tradition. He became interested in super-heroes early with the Ninja Turtles, Transformers, and Power Rangers. He also became a Superman fan (fortunately, there were TV reruns of the "real" Superman from my youth). Brett had a pair of pajamas made to look like a Superman suit. Since he wore them during a growth-spurt year, the bottom of the pants came almost to his knees when they were finally retired.

All the super-heroes were just not quite super enough for Brett, however. As a gifted artist, he began drawing his own super-heroes. They possessed different powers and gadgets that made each uniquely super.

After he had gone to bed one night, I went into his room and found him lying on top of the covers, dressed in his Superman PJ's, and staring at the ceiling in deep thought. He let me know what was on his mind.

"Dad, is God everywhere?"
Yes, Brett, God is everywhere."
"Does God know everything?"
"Yes, son, he knows everything."
"Can he do anything?"
"Yes, he can do anything."

Suddenly it dawned on Brett that all the super-heroes of TV and his imagination were still not super enough. He sighed and said, "I WISH I WAS GOD."

The Psalmist asked, "What is man that you are mindful of him?" (Psalms 8:4). When you are out at night, far from the city lights, perhaps camping under the stars, do you look up into the vastness of the universe and ask a similar question: Who am I, a speck in all creation, that you, O God, are mindful of me?

God is not only mindful; he has given us the ability to know him, as well. Beyond that, he offers us his strength, his power, and his wisdom. Furthermore, God sent his only Son to be our example, so that we can know him as the Son of Man. The Son was given, not only as an example, but also as a sacrifice—to pay the dept of sin that we could never pay. Thereby, we can have fellowship with a Holy God.

Although we cannot be God, we can know God in us. Forget super-heroes! Forget Superman! We can know GOD IN US!

How can that be possible? It is possible through a relationship and discipleship with Jesus Christ. Just as Brett and I dressed like Superman to imitate our hero, we can be like Christ by imitating him. Do not be misled, however. This is not accomplished through our human efforts or through an act of our imagination, or by the concept of mind over matter. It is accomplished through the supernatural, transforming power and love of the God who created us. It is accomplished through faith in Jesus Christ as the Son of God.

These supernatural abilities were not born in us when we entered the world. This gift of God's indwelling Spirit is accomplished when we are "born again" into his Kingdom.

> *Therefore, if anyone is in Christ, he is a new creation; the old has gone, the new has come! ... We are therefore Christ's ambassadors, as though God were making his appeal through us. (2 Corinthians 5:17,20)*

We are born again as a "new creation", and the transformation begins by the "renewing of our minds" (Romans 12:2).

Jesus said, "The Kingdom of God is within you." He also said,

> *"The Kingdom of Heaven is like treasure hidden in a field. When a man found it, he hid it again, and then in his joy went and sold all he had and bought that field." (Matthew 13:44)*

God will impart his all in us when we give our all to him. It is the most SUPER deal in the universe.

YOUR TURN:

(1) When have you experienced the supernatural power of God?
(2) Please read a chapter of Acts. Were these early disciples acting under their own power?
(3) Is there anything in your life blocking the "power connection"?
(4) Pray for his supernatural power to manifest itself in you.

CHAPTER 30

THE TAR BABY

But who are you, O man, to talk back to God? "Shall what is formed say to him who formed it, 'Why did you make me like this?'"

Romans 9:20

My fourth year of life was a good one. Several monumental events of that year are deeply etched into that year's memory vault. That was the year I first rode a bike without training wheels. We got a new black and white television to watch Captain Kangaroo. When my mom left the kitchen for a few minutes, I ate a mixing bowl of cake batter. Dagwood made famous the "Dagwood sandwich", and I copied his creation with a six-layer masterpiece. My hands were scorched when I wrapped them around the muffler of the lawnmower (after my dad had warned me not to touch it). My finger was sliced when I stuck it in a neighbor's new bike siren. Another finger was sliced when I showed my inquiring friends how it happened.

The coup de grace, however, occurred on a hot summer day when all of us kids were playing outside in summer attire (barefoot, shorts, and no shirt). Excitement was in the air, because the street was being paved. Watching the large, loud, smelly, smoky road equipment provided great entertainment.

The paving was done by scraping the existing surface, laying down a layer of tar, and spreading gravel atop the tar. After the workers were finished, I went out to the edge of the street and sat down. Much of the tar had oozed out from the side, and the summer sun had kept it the consistency of molasses.

By chance, I had recently heard the Uncle Remus story, "The Tar Baby". Finding a stick, I proceeded to transform myself into the Tar Baby. Dabbing and twisting the stick into the gooey tar, I loaded it up and smeared it onto every exposed area of skin I could reach. Since I only had on a pair of shorts, my coverage was pretty complete.

Having finished my childhood make-over, I ran inside to my mom and announced, "Look, Mom, I'm the Tar Baby!" Mom was not amused. Thankfully, an aunt happened to be visiting at the time, and her hysterical laughter saved me. It took quite a bit of soaking and scrubbing with kerosene, but the tar did come off, and there seems to be no traces remaining.

Mom forgave me. Hopefully, she thinks of the event now with amusement.

Who did you want to be when you were young? Was there a famous person who you secretly admired and longed to be? Was there, perhaps, a friend that seemed to have it all, and you privately wanted to trade places? Did you want to have different color hair or different color eyes? Did you want to be taller or shorter? Did you want to be slimmer or more muscular?

We all at some time have wanted to be someone we're not. Since the actual transformation cannot occur, we resort to imitation, covetousness, or jealousy.

The phrase "all men are created equal" was used by our country's Founding Fathers in the Declaration of Independence. The intent of the authors, in my understanding, was to convey that we are created equal "under the law". Of course, that part of the statement was omitted, and the phrase is often quoted as absolute truth.

If we were all created equal, then why do we desire to be like someone else? Certainly the belief that we are all created equal ignores the obvious and is also unbiblical. We simply are not the same in intelligence, appearance, talents, abilities, gifts, or physical make-up.

Jesus told the parable about the master who gave three of his servants varying degrees of money to steward while he took a trip. This parable not only teaches us a lesson in stewardship, but, also, it teaches us that we receive varying amounts of "talents" from our heavenly Master.

Please don't confuse inequality by worldly standards, though, with God's all-encompassing love for each of his children. We are all loved equally by God. We are all covered equally by his mercy and grace. The gift of salvation is offered equally to us all, because we are each valued equally in his sight.

We are, nevertheless, created different from one another by our creator for a unique purpose. With that Godly purpose—whether it is serving, teaching, encouraging, contributing to the needs of others, leading, or showing mercy—we are gifted according to the measure God determines.

> *Just as each of us has one body with many members, and these members do not all have the same function, so in Christ we who are many form one body, and each member belongs to all the others. We have different gifts, **according to the grace given us**. (Romans 12:4–6)*

Furthermore, since many varying members form one body in Christ, we recognize the many different functions of each member. Although not equal in themselves, they are equally important in the formation of the whole. It is not a matter of our deciding but a matter of God's purpose that gives each member its function.

> *Now the body is not made up of one part but of many . . . God has arranged the parts in the body, every one of them, just as he wanted them to be . . . Now you are the body of Christ, and each of you is a part of it. (1 Corinthians 12:14, 18, 27)*

The story is told of a handful of clay taken from a riverbank. The clay had great aspirations. It knew its destiny was to be molded and shaped into a fine gilded urn, gracing the palace of a king. After being turned and formed on the potter's wheel, baked in a fiery furnace to harden, and placed on a shelf to cool, the handful of clay saw what it had become, reflected in a vat of water. The reflection was not of a gilded urn, but of an ugly, red flowerpot.

The handful of clay was devastated. Dirt was thrown into the pot the following day, and the handful of clay was even more distraught. Noticing another ugly, red flowerpot beside it, the disillusioned clay asked, "Why are we just ugly flowerpots full of dirt? I wasn't supposed to be this. I was supposed to be made into something grand and magnificent!"

The neighboring flowerpot explained, "We're made only to be a vessel. But beautiful white lilies will be planted inside us, and we will be grand and magnificent, not because of what we are, but because of what lives within us."

We are like a handful of clay. Some of us are formed for highly visible, exalted positions, while others are fashioned for unseen, lowly service. Yet, we cannot always accept this, and we cry out in protest, "Why did you make me like this?"

> *But who are you, O man, to talk back to God? "Shall what is formed say to him who formed it, 'Why did you make me like this?'" Does not the potter have the right to make out of the same lump of clay some pottery for noble purposes and some for common use? (Romans 9:20–21)*

Accepting the way our creator made us confirms our belief in the sovereignty of God. It further confirms our trust in God's ability to use us exactly as he intends for his purpose. Instead of spending our life hoping in vain to be someone we're not, we should be spending our life being used for the service he intended.

YOUR TURN:

(1) What would you like to change about the way you were made?
(2) Can you change it?
(3) Can you accept it and move on and understand that God made you as he saw fit?
(4) How can you take a "handicap" and let it be used by the Lord?
(5) Think of someone who was "nothing" by worldly standards, yet, was used mightily by God.
(6) Pray for acceptance of how you were made. Know that God will use you.

Part Twelve

His Amazing Grace

CHAPTER 31

LEE

In him we have redemption through his blood, the forgiveness of sins, in accordance with the riches of God's grace that he lavished on us with all wisdom and understanding.
Ephesians 1:7–8

God sometimes, as Oswald Chambers often said, "engineers our circumstances". He will put us in a particular place at a particular time to be used as one of his instruments on earth. We also refer to "divine appointments" when God causes us to cross the path of another at just the opportune time to be used as a messenger, encourager, or witness. One Sunday afternoon God engineered my circumstances and gave me a divine appointment.

A meeting of Sunday school teachers and leaders was held at my church. As was my habit, I drove my car around back of the church to a gravel parking lot. While putting the gearshift in "park", I decided not to park there and drove around to a parking lot on another side. Although this was a strange thing for me to do, especially since I had to walk further to the meeting room, I didn't give it much thought at the time.

Following the meeting I walked across the parking lot toward my car. I noticed a man approaching me from my right. As we intersected I spoke to him and stopped, since he appeared to have a question.

He was obviously a homeless man. His hair was stringy and unkempt. The clothes he wore were dirty and tattered. He smelled of sweat, tobacco, and alcohol. Around his shoulder hung a backpack in which, I presumed, he kept all his possessions.

Pointing to the church he asked, "What's going on here?"

I mumbled something about a meeting, but inside my heart I knew that God had put this man in my path for a reason. I asked the man to sit with me on the steps of an old house by the church used for Sunday school classes. After introducing myself he gave me his name, Lee.

Lee began sharing with me a little about his life. He had come to the area five or six years ago in order to be treated for alcoholism. The treatment worked for a while, but for years Lee had wandered the streets ever in search of the next drink. He was wandering that Sunday afternoon and looking for a place to spend the evening with a bottle.

While we sat on the steps I began sharing with him a little about my life. I told him from experience that he didn't have to live the way he was living. I told him that God was a God of love, and that Christ had died for the forgiveness of our sins. I told him that God could so transform his life that he wouldn't recognize himself.

Lee's attention was suddenly diverted as he looked down at his backpack placed by his feet. The cloth bottom was wet and a clear liquid had run out onto the ground. He frantically opened the pack and reached inside to determine the source of the leak. It was his water bottle, and his face showed the relief. He pulled out another bottle, a bottle of vodka. He had been concerned that the leak had come from the object of his greatest desire.

No longer did he want to talk with me. He stood up and said, "All I want right now is to finish off this bottle. I'll think about what you said later."

He began to walk away but looked back at me one last time. In his eyes I saw a man who was empty . . . and lost.

When I got in my car I could only sit there and wonder. How did Lee get where he is now? Maybe he started out as a young man known to have great potential. Maybe he was voted "most likely to succeed". Maybe he won scholarships to college and there met the girl of his dreams. Maybe while at college a buddy approached him at a party and handed him a bottle of beer and said, "Drink up! This is college! Have fun!" And so he did.

Maybe after college he married that girl of his dreams, had a great job and career, even had a couple of kids. Along the way, however, Lee never put down the bottle. His drinking consumed him and his family. Maybe he lost his job to alcohol, and his wife could take the drunken days and lonely nights no longer. Maybe she gave him an ultimatum, "It's either the bottle or your family . . .", and Lee took the bottle and walked away . . . just as he had done with me a few moments before.

Sitting in my car I realized with no doubt whatsoever that only one thing separated Lee from myself—GOD'S AMAZING GRACE.

Before Lee walked away I gave him my name and phone number. One evening a couple of weeks later I received a phone call. It was Lee. He had found a small homeless shelter in which to stay for a while and was out of the elements. I asked if I could see him the next day (it so happened, not by coincidence, but by divine intervention, that I had already scheduled to be off work for a doctor's appointment), and he agreed.

The next morning we met, and I gave him a Bible that my daughter, Kellie, had given me for that purpose. Again we talked, and I pleaded with him to accept God's free gift of salvation and experience a new life in Christ. How much I wanted him to know what his life could become!

How wonderful it would be if I could tell you that Lee found salvation that day and has since lived a victorious life. But he walked away from me again, saying that he just wasn't ready. He would think about it—later. This time he didn't look back, but at least he held a Bible and not a bottle.

―――

That was the last time I saw Lee. Attempts to find him after that meeting were in vain. I have not stopped praying for

Lee, and I have not stopped hoping that he will lay down the bottle for the Cross of Christ.

Lee taught me and reminded me. Many are those who are empty and lost and are absolutely helpless to help themselves. However, I am also convinced that absolutely no one is hopeless, because no one is beyond the reach of GOD'S AMAZING GRACE.

Pray for Lee.

YOUR TURN:

(1) Where would you be today were it not for God's amazing grace?
(2) Take the time right now to thank him for that grace.
(3) Recite and apply the words of the hymn, "Amazing Grace".
(4) Please take the time to pray for Lee.

CHAPTER 32

THE FINAL INNING

*"These men who were hired last worked only one hour,"
they said, "and you have made them equal to us who have
borne the burden of the work, and the heat of the day."*
                                    Matthew 20:12

Some of you may remember the events and circumstances of the year I'll describe. Can you recall what year it was?

Mom would give me a quarter and tell me to walk downtown to "The Clipper" barbershop and get a haircut. She didn't know that I had discovered another barbershop that only charged fifteen cents. With the dime I had left over I would buy a soda or candy bar or ten flat packs of bubble gum on the way home.

The haircut was always the same, a flattop, which was also the style worn by my boyhood heroes. The heroes were pictured on cards found in those penny packs of flat bubble gum. My friends and I collected those cards, and I remember having the cards of the greatest heroes of that summer—Roger Maris and Mickey Mantle.

The year was 1961, and Maris and Mantle were both New York Yankee baseball players. Each was slugging it out in an attempt to break Babe Ruth's single season homerun record of sixty. Most of my friends were Maris fans, but I remember rooting for Mickey Mantle, probably because he was the underdog.

The 1961 baseball season ended with Maris breaking Ruth's record with sixty-one homeruns. Mantle finished with fifty-four.

That's about all I knew of the man Mantle until I heard about his public battle with alcoholism and his battle with liver cancer in the 1990's. Recently he died when he could not win the battle with cancer.

Just the other day, while walking by the stand where witnessing tracts are kept in our church, I spotted the familiar face and flattop of my boyhood hero on the cover of one of the tracts. I picked one up and began reading about the life of Mickey Mantle off the baseball field.

Mantle left Oklahoma for New York at the age of 19. His dad died at age 40 after Mickey's first season. The disease that took his father's life, Hodgkin's disease, had also taken his grandfather's and two uncles' lives, all before age 40.

Since Hodgkin's is a genetic disease Mickey was convinced that he also was destined to die young, so he partied hard and lived like there was no tomorrow. He made the statement later in his life that he didn't care for his body because he never thought he would be old. He lived well past his own expectations, however.

Finally in 1994 he sought treatment for alcoholism, but he knew something was still missing in his life. In 1995 cancer was discovered in his liver. A liver transplant was performed and it seemed for a while like Mickey would be around for another inning. But it would soon be realized that the cancer had spread, and Mickey's days were numbered.

He called an old friend, second baseman Bobby Richardson, a committed Christian. Bobby went to the hospital room and listened as Mickey shared the news. He had accepted the free gift of salvation offered by Jesus Christ.

In his final inning Mickey Mantle knew the greatest victory of his life—a victory not won by himself on the baseball field, but given by a Savior on a hill called Calvary. And what mattered most was not that his name was written in the Hall of Fame, but that his name was written in the Book of Life.

Mickey Mantle has a legacy as one of the greatest baseball players of all time. His greater legacy will be those reached for Christ, because his face is on the cover and his testimony is contained within that witnessing tract. That is an eternal legacy.

YOUR TURN:

(1) Have you known anyone who experienced a late-life or deathbed conversion?
(2) Have you heard a late-life convert make the statement, "I only regret not coming to know Christ earlier in my life"?
(3) Are you waiting to make a commitment? Why?
(4) Are there jealousies by other Christians from these late-life conversions? (Please read Matthew 20:12, Luke 15:25–30)
(5) Pray for someone you know who needs to meet and know Christ.

CHAPTER 33

2000

Serve the Lord with gladness . . .

Psalms 100:2

Some things over the years haven't changed much with me. My deepest thinking is still done while fishing (especially when the fish aren't biting). On a fishing day at Mr. Craig's farm pond when I was 11 or 12 years old, I vividly recall doing some deep thinking.

My deep thoughts of that day involved the pondering, for the first time, of the next century. Since it was the year 1965, I began to do some calculations. With my math skills I figured that the year 2000 would be thirty-five years in the future. Again employing my skills with numbers, I calculated that in the year 2000 I would become 47 years old. My dwelling on the subject didn't last long, however. Either the fish started biting, or I determined that thirty-five years was practically an eternity. Furthermore, I could not imagine being 47 years old. Never would I be THAT old!

It's now the year 2000. Thirty-five years wasn't an eternity (it seemed to have passed in the blink of an eye), and I am THAT old. My first thoughts about this year never included the terms "Y2K" or the "New Millennium". Nevertheless, here I am at this point in time.

On a recent fishing trip I did some more deep thinking. My thoughts involved the searching for a word, one word I could use to describe my journey into the new millennium. The word I chose was gladness—GLADNESS.

When I look back over my life, I see its beginnings in the care and nurturing of a Christian mom and dad. I'm so glad I had them then and still have them today. When I think of how they also prepared me to hear the call of God's Holy Spirit, I'm so glad.

When I consider that God spoke to me at the age of eight and that through my belief in Christ I was born again and became a part of God's family, I'm so glad.

When I recall the girl I met in my 20's that said, "Yes"; and after I said, "I do", I've known the gift of a loving and devoted wife named Jill, I'm so glad.

When I see the faces of our three children, Meagan, Brett, and Kellie, I know that they, too, are a precious gift from God. They make me so glad.

When I think of friendships and relationships closer than brothers, and know that they will endure for eternity, I'm so glad.

When I consider the extent of God's love for me; when I consider how much he has forgiven; when I think of his mercy and grace; when I consider how much he has blessed, I AM SO GLAD.

This week I read about a button that was given to children upon graduation from Vacation Bible School. On the button were these letters:

GIFWMY

It stands for, "GOD ISN'T FINISHED WITH ME YET".

This is my last thought today: God isn't finished with me yet. **I'm so glad**.

YOUR TURN:

(1) Look up "gladness" in your Bible. Notice the many times it is connected with the word "joy". Why are they connected?
(2) List five reasons you have for gladness.
(3) Serve the Lord with gladness.
(4) Pray that God will show you why you should be glad today.

Part Thirteen

True Riches

CHAPTER 34

WHO WANTS TO BE A MILLIONAIRE

Do not store up for yourselves treasures on earth, where moth and rust destroy, and where thieves break in and steal. But store up for yourselves treasures in heaven, where moth and rust do not destroy, and where thieves do not break in and steal. For where your treasure is, there your heart will be also.

Matthew 6:19–21

Most of us have watched the show, "Who Wants to be a Millionaire". We see contestants who, by choosing the right answers to multiple-choice questions, can walk away with as much as a million dollars. We're fascinated by the drama, by the strategy of using "lifelines", by the sometimes greed of the players, by the wit of the host, and by the risks we see people take. But more than that, we're fascinated by the prospect of instant wealth.

Our fascination with instant wealth goes beyond this show and others like it. The lure extends to many areas of our society and goes beyond fascination. Often it leads to obsession, not only for instant wealth but also for extreme wealth.

We see people lined up for blocks waiting to buy lottery tickets for that miniscule chance of instant wealth. Many of these same people are spending money that should be spent on groceries for their family or clothes for their children, but the obsession for wealth is too strong.

We read about sports figures, many still in their teens, signing contracts worth tens of millions of dollars. Then we pay inflated ticket prices to see these idols play.

We are obsessed with instant and extreme wealth garnered from the stock market. Pictures of the new dot-com millionaires or billionaires are on every business or investment magazine. And we want to hop on board the train leaving the station in hopes of riding it to wealth.

This obsession with wealth is hardly new or unique to our time. A rich young man walked up to Jesus with this question: "What must I do to inherit eternal life?" When Jesus gave his answer it involved something the rich young man could not do, give up his millions. He chose his earthly wealth instead of discipleship with Christ and eternal life. Jesus observed,

> "How hard it is for the rich to enter the Kingdom of God." (Mark 10:23)

True Riches

When your children ask you, "Mom, Dad, do you want to be rich?" How do you answer them?

The Apostle Paul speaks of "the unsearchable riches of Christ" in Ephesians 3:8. Also in Philippians 4:19 he adds assurance that "my God will meet all your needs according to his glorious riches in Christ Jesus."

So as Christians we should be able to answer our children, "I'm already rich!" and exemplify it by living the words of the hymn:

I'd rather have Jesus than silver or gold.
I'd rather have him than have riches untold.
I'd rather have Jesus than anything . . .
This old world affords today.

YOUR TURN:

(1) Have you been guilty of wanting to achieve instant, unearned wealth?
(2) Have you played the stock market, not as a long-term investment, but as a desire for quick wealth?
(3) Do you buy lottery tickets?
(4) What example does this set for your children?
(5) Please read Matthew 6:19–21.
(6) Pray for understanding of true riches.

CHAPTER 35

DROP THE BAG

But God said to him, "You fool! This very night your life will be demanded from you."
Luke 12:20

Saturday morning was MY morning. School was put on hold for a while, and, since I was only about eight years old, work had not yet entered the picture. I'd grab a bowl, a box of cereal, and a carton of milk and park myself in front of our black and white TV set. Weekdays I had to suffer through my mom's breakfasts of scrambled eggs, biscuits and gravy, sausage, and grits. What a treat to sit and gorge myself on cold cereal (how my tastes have changed!).

Back in the medieval period of television, the late 50's and early 60's, there were only three or four stations available to watch in our area. Saturday morning viewing for most kids consisted of cartoons, and I watched my share. But my favorite Saturday morning viewing was the classic Tarzan episodes, starring Johnny Weissmuller.

Those old Tarzan movies really pricked my childhood imagination and, of course, led to some creative role-playing. Vines would be found in the neighborhood over creeks and gullies, and a shirtless, short pant, barefoot Tarzan-wannabee boy would fly across the abyss with the jungle cry, "AHHH-AH-AHH-AH-AHAHAHAH-AHAH-AHAH." The other players needed for my adventures would be recruited. A girl friend would be Jane. Some other friends would be the natives. The youngest kid would be Boy. It was always difficult to find a volunteer to be Cheetah, however.

How I loved watching those old Tarzan movies! A particular one remains in my memory more than any of the others. The theme was probably repeated in more than one episode and was certainly seen in other movies before and since.

The adventure begins with a band of "white hunters" who have come to Africa for a safari. The hunters are wealthy Englishmen and are decked out in the latest safari fashion. Their pants are ballooned in the thighs and tucked into high leather boots. Around their waists are wide leather belts with a holstered pistol on the side. Topping off the outfit is the famous safari hat. In a long caravan behind these hunters can be seen the native porters and beasts of burden carrying all their supplies and equipment.

The white hunters accidentally stumble across a tribal civilization hidden back in a mountainous area of the jungle. It is discovered that this civilization has mined gold, silver, and jewels from the mountains, and the king is adorned with some of the shiny metal and sparkling stones. A cache of the treasure is stored in a nearby guarded cave. The Englishmen begin their scheming.

A diversionary tactic is used to distract the natives, and the thieves make their move. They enter the cave and begin filling up canvas bags with gold, silver, and jewels. Tarzan, meanwhile, has gotten wind of the scheme and is vine swinging and yelling his way through the jungle.

The men exit the caves with their bags of treasure and begin running along the narrow mountain trail above the sheer cliffs. They round a bend and find a deep gorge separating them from the mountain beyond. A bridge, however, made of twine and sticks links the two mountains. The movie camera pans to the bottom of the gorge to show a river teeming with crocodiles waiting for their next meal.

Scampering across the bridge, the thieves try to escape. The last thief on the bridge looks back to see Tarzan closing fast. Suddenly the sticks below his feet break, and he falls through the bridge. Desperately he grabs the rope framework with one hand as he falls. With his other hand he is still clutching the canvas bag of treasure.

Tarzan reaches the spot where the man is swaying in mid-air and tries to hoist him back onto the bridge. "Drop the bag!" Tarzan implores. The bag is heavy, laden with gold, silver, and jewels, and it keeps Tarzan, despite his incredible strength, from pulling the man back onto the bridge. The bag of treasure also keeps the man from using his other hand to grasp Tarzan's hand and be pulled to safety.

"Drop the bag!" Tarzan yells again. The man looks at the bag, looks up at Tarzan, and looks down at the bag again. He can't do it. He can't drop the bag! It's the treasure of a lifetime! Slowly, the grip of his hand on the rope begins to loosen, and he falls screaming to the river below. The next scene is the frantic thrashing of crocodiles around a bundle of safari fashion.

While the exact details of this Tarzan episode may not be accurately recorded in my memory, the moral impact of the story was certain: Even though his very life depended on it, the great white hunter couldn't DROP THE BAG.

This theme is not unique to that particular Tarzan adventure. It is a recurring theme in countless movies and novels. It is a theme that occurs daily in real life. While in real life there may not be a dramatic last-minute event that has us hanging onto life with one hand and holding onto our treasures of a lifetime with the other, there are the daily decisions and choices that lead to the same conclusion.

We can go back to Jesus' day and find the account of one such choice. In Matthew 19, we read about a rich young man who approached Jesus with a question:

"Teacher, what good thing must I do to get eternal life?"

Jesus first replied that he must keep the commandments. The rich young man assured Jesus that he kept the commandments, but he wanted to know,

True Riches

"What do I still lack?"

Jesus answered,

"If you want to be perfect, go, sell your possessions and give to the poor, and you will have treasure in heaven. Then come, follow me." (Matthew 19:16–21)

Picture this young man reaching out with one hand in hopes of finding eternal life, while in the other hand holding the bag with his treasures. He had a clear choice between everlasting life and the bag. He had to make a decision between walking with Jesus, the Son of God, and the bag.

The encounter concludes as the man "went away sad". He couldn't DROP THE BAG. The scenario has not changed in 2000 years.

Jesus tells us in one of those paradoxes of discipleship:

"For whoever wants to save his life will lose it, but whoever loses his life for me and for the gospel will find it."

He then asks one of the most compelling questions ever asked:

"What good is it for a man to gain the whole world, yet forfeit his soul?" (Mark 8:34–36)

Jesus offers us life—abundant life in this world and eternal life in the world to come. Yet, so many will not know it, because they cannot let go of their shiny, sparkling treasures.

Jesus is saying, DROP THE BAG. Lose the things of earth that "moth and rust destroy, and where thieves break in and steal". Lose your life "for my sake" and I will give you "treasures in heaven".

Jesus is saying, DROP THE BAG, because,

"No one can serve two masters. Either he will hate the one and love the other, or he will be devoted to the one and despise the other. You cannot serve both God and money."
(Matthew 6:24)

YOUR TURN:

(1) What "bag" are you holding onto?
(2) What do you consider your treasures?
(3) Do you really believe Matthew 6:24?
(4) Do you serve money or is money your servant?
(5) Do you need to "drop the bag" in order to follow Christ?
(6) Please read Luke 12:13–21.
(7) Please read Matthew 19:16–30.
(8) Pray that God will reveal your "bag".

CHAPTER 36

LIFESTYLES

You have let go of the commands of God and are holding on to the traditions of men.

Mark 7:8

Home restoration, renovation, and remodeling shows have become a popular television theme. They are a favorite of mine, because I imagine myself to be a handyman (no one else would agree), and these shows provide helpful tips.

A typical episode of a house remodeling show would follow a scenario similar to the following story. Bob and Suzie are a well educated couple in their 30's with two children ages four and seven. Bob is a commercial architect, and Suzie has an upscale boutique. They live in a manicured, suburban neighborhood. As they sit in their comfortable living room, the host of the show begins to ask questions to assess their desires in the remodel.

Out of A Distant Land

Bob wants a space he can call his own. He wants to be able to display his collection of old tools, have a place for his gym and workout equipment, and just have a retreat for listening to the new stereo system they plan to add.

Suzie wants a modern kitchen with all the bells and whistles. She also wants to "open up" the floor plan to allow for the entertaining they like to do. The master suite needs to have large his-and-hers walk-in closets, a sitting room, and a large bath with a whirlpool tub so she can "pamper" herself.

The list of "wants" grows as the show progresses and so does the bottom line on cost. The budget for the remodel was certainly not written in stone, and the bank is happy to accommodate a larger loan.

At some point in the show, the question is asked, "What is the reason you want to remodel?" The common answer would be along these lines: "We feel the house has gotten a little dated. We need more room to entertain. We just want a house that better suits our LIFESTYLE."

It is a buzzword of our society. Television shows are dedicated to it. Newspapers have separate sections devoted to it. Magazines thrive on the many derivations of it. Houses and communities are built around it. Vehicles are manufactured specifically to accommodate it. Fashion centers upon it. It controls us. It is our master—LIFESTYLE.

Lifestyle is a strange concept and cannot be defined in specific terms. I checked a Webster's Dictionary printed in

1967 to seek a definition. The word listing went from "life size" to "lifetime". No "lifestyle" was found. Nevertheless, this is not a development or concept that has occurred only within the last 30 years. We have simply given it a name, elevated it to deity status, and worship it as our master.

Lifestyle varies according to several factors: income level, education, profession, geography, expectations, social status (actually, social status may be considered somewhat of a goal of lifestyle), debt, family tradition, and, even, sexual "orientation".

While it may vary according to these factors, lifestyle is inherently a choice. Hence, we have the term, **lifestyle choice**. We are not forced into a lifestyle by any of the above-mentioned variables. We choose a lifestyle that fits our priorities and goals in life. Often the choice is not made with care or with much thought; instead, the choice is usually made progressively.

A certain lifestyle lures us, perhaps from images in a magazine or a television show. Maybe our friends and associates enjoy a lifestyle that attracts us. Like a seductress, it wraps around us and pulls us into its grasp. We, then, become captive to that lifestyle.

Lifestyle is, essentially, a **style of life** that we use as a framework or foundation upon which we make decisions that affect every aspect of our life. Looking at Bob and Suzie from the opening story, we can see some examples of this.

Progressing up the social and career ladders, Bob and Suzie have all the outward appearances of success. Their friends and business associates are at their level of success or above, and, as a result, they feel the need to adjust their style of life to fit this higher rung in the social ladder. Their house needs "updating" with the latest in appliances, electronics, and décor. Spaciousness is important to allow for entertaining. The utmost in creature comforts accommodate the need for "pampering". Their lifestyle framework extends beyond the house, however.

Let's suppose this same couple feels the need, after a stressful week at work, to join their friends at the lake. A new ski boat with all the accessories and, possibly, a lake cabin would be a requirement. Towing the ski boat and all the gear would, of course, mandate the latest behemoth sport utility vehicle.

Adding to this lifestyle list would be the necessary clubs and organizations to which Bob and Suzie must belong. It is, after all, very important to be seen in the proper settings. One of those organizations happens to be the church. Careful consideration is given to the church, because it must not be a church that demands a binding commitment of time and energy. Certainly they are willing to give one or two Sunday mornings each month for "religious activities". After all, it is good for image, business, and the kids.

Did I mention this couple has two children? They, also, hold great importance to Bob and Suzie, and much effort is made to fit them into their lifestyle. The children will make careful notes from their parent's example and seek their own lifestyles accordingly (they, however, will want the lifestyle earlier in their marriage and simply finance it with borrowed money).

Notice that practically all of this couple's choices fit into the framework of their lifestyle choice. Now answer this question: Is there a slave-master relationship in effect here? Who is the slave? What is the master?

To answer that question, let's look at another aspect of this couple's choice. How is this lifestyle **maintained**? Do resources that have been saved over the years allow them to maintain this style of life? Or do debts that grow increasingly voluminous maintain it? Furthermore, what is traded to maintain this lifestyle?

Bob and Suzie trade the most valuable resource any of us have—**time**—for the lifestyle they value so deeply. They both work long hours to earn the money to pay the bills to support the fragile framework of their precious lifestyle.

Who is the **slave**? What is the **master**?

As followers of Christ, we are faced with a lifestyle choice, and we need to choose it carefully. Too many, calling the name of Christ, are ingrained in today's culture and choose a "LIFESTYLE CHRISTIANITY". We should be choosing, instead, a LIFE STYLED AS CHRIST'S DISCIPLE.

We can choose by listening to the seductive call of the world, or we can choose by listening to the instructions found in his Word. Hear this from his Word:

> *Do not conform any longer to the pattern of this world, but be transformed by the renewing of your mind. Then you will be able to test and approve what God's will is—his good, pleasing and perfect will. (Romans 12:2)*

YOUR TURN:

(1) Would you describe Bob and Suzie's lifestyle as "living the American dream"?
(2) Is the "American dream" compatible with Christian discipleship?
(3) Have we altered discipleship to fit our culture?
(4) If you tithe 10%, are you, then, as a Christian, free to spend the other 90% as you please?
(5) How does stewardship apply to lifestyle slavery?
(6) Can you serve two masters?
(7) Pray that your style of life will reflect discipleship in Christ.

CHAPTER 37

I NEED

Look at the birds of the air; they do not sow or reap or store away in barns, and yet your heavenly Father feeds them. Are you not much more valuable than they?
                                                              Matthew 6:26

When our older daughter Meagan was about four years old, she spent a weekend at my parents' home. My mom took her to a local department store, and, of course, Meagan headed straight for the aisle with the dolls. She looked over the display of hundreds of dolls and finally saw just the one for her. Looking up at my mom with those big blue eyes she said, "Grandmom, **I need** that doll."

Meagan knew, even at age four, that there was a difference between her wants and her needs. Wants were not always satisfied, but needs were. She also knew that Grandmom loved her and would certainly satisfy her needs. Meagan walked out of the store that day with her needed new doll.

I'm not above using that same technique myself. Many times when I sense the mood is right, I'll very lovingly take my wife's hand, look deeply into her eyes, and say with great feeling, "Jill, Honey, I NEED . . . to hold . . . a trout." Of course, she loves me and desires to satisfy my needs. So she lovingly responds, "Why don't you just go fishing!"

What are our real needs, and how are they satisfied? There are the needs of the body, and Jesus addressed those in Matthew 6. He spoke of how the Father gives food and drink to the birds of the air and clothes the lilies of the field. Jesus assures us that the Father knows we need these things. But Jesus always goes to the core of our desires and addresses the needs of the soul, the needs of the heart.

What is the real need of a society that seems only to seek more of the material comforts and pleasures? What is the real need of a person addicted to alcohol or other drugs, lust, or power? What is the real need of a teenage boy who kills his classmates for revenge? What is the real need of each heart?

Unfortunately, we often look to the wants of this world to satisfy the needs of the heart. Read the finding of the writer of Ecclesiastes:

I denied myself nothing my eyes desired;
I refused my heart no pleasure.
My heart took delight in all my work,
And this was the reward for all my labor.
Yet when I surveyed all that my hands had done
And what I had toiled to achieve,

True Riches

Everything was meaningless; a chasing after the wind;
Nothing was gained under the sun.
Eccleesiastes 2:10–11

In spite of all our searching, there is only one thing that will satisfy the needs of our heart—**A relationship with Jesus Christ.** All our real needs—love, hope, meaning, purpose, peace, clarity, friendship, calmness, assurance, significance—are met in a personal relationship with Jesus Christ.

There are many needs that we can try to satisfy alone, but the real need of the heart is not one of them. Jesus summarizes his teaching concerning our needs with this command:

"But seek first his kingdom and his righteousness (our heart's real need), and all these things (our physical needs) will be given to you as well." (Matthew 6:33)

YOUR TURN:

(1) Will putting the Kingdom of God first in our life balance our wants with our needs? Think about it.
(2) Do you pray for wants or for needs?
(3) In our "land of plenty" are we blinded to the difference between wants and needs?
(4) Pray that God will open your eyes to your true need.

CHAPTER 38

IS IT IN YOU

My joy knows no bounds.
                                        2 Corinthians 7:4

The marketing of products is a fascinating subject. While I never took a single marketing course in college, I would certainly recommend it to my children. Marketing is simply the attractive presentation of a product to be sold in the marketplace. We commonly refer to this presentation as advertising. The fascination comes from the method of presentation.

My challenge in viewing advertising is trying to determine two basic ingredients: the group of people targeted by the advertising (young, old, boomer, ethnicity, wealthy, blue collar, white collar, struggling college student, etc.) and the emotional appeal (snob or better-than-the-neighbor's, sentimentality, fatherhood, motherhood, outrageous happiness). At times, of course, a company will not show its products at all in an advertisement. It will, instead, tout the great things it is doing with some of the money you spend on its products, usually related, somehow, to its being kind to the environment or to helping inner-city kids. That kind of corporate "window dressing" makes us feel good about buying their merchandise when we go to the store (notice especially these "we-do-so-many-great-things" advertisements from the tobacco and alcohol industries).

Let's take two products with which we are all familiar and pose a question relating to our spiritual condition. The first product is a dishwashing detergent that has been around as long as I can remember. Try to imagine the group of marketers as they prepared to launch this product.

"OK, guys, what can we name this detergent that will really grab the consumer?"

"We need to name it something that will make people happy just thinking about doing the dishes. How about, 'HAPPY'?"

"Nah, happiness is too fickle and fleeting. I know! Let's call it 'JOY'!"

Thus was born the dishwashing detergent that always gives us that abiding presence of JOY whenever we wash dishes. Smart marketing, huh?

Then there's the so-called "sports drink" that quenches thirst and replaces what we lose in sweat (there was a time we thought sweat was good riddance). It also has been around for a long time. I remember first drinking it at football practice in high school. Back then it only came in one flavor—orange. Actually, it was more the color orange than the flavor.

The company now making this drink has some pretty slick advertising. Athletes of various sports are shown in the midst of extreme exertion and are sweating (the female athletes perspire) profusely as the colors of various flavors of the sport drink—blue, orange, green, purple—bead up and run down their bodies. Then the question is asked, "IS IT IN YOU?"

Let's combine these two products and their marketing techniques and pose a question relating to us as Christian disciples: JOY! IS IT IN YOU?

When unbelievers watch the procession of Christians on Sunday morning as we enter the church, or on Monday morning as we enter the workplace, are they able to see the joy that is in us? Or do they see a group of stodgy men and women, with furrowed brows and the weight of the world on their shoulders, seemingly void of that ingredient that is supposed to permeate the Christian's soul and manifest itself in attitude and countenance?

The Founding Fathers regrettably used a phrase in the Declaration of Independence referring to our "inalienable right" to the "pursuit of happiness". It is that "pursuit of happiness" that so often permeates our soul.

Ask a graduating high school or college student what plans they have for their life, and, inevitably, the desire will emerge, "I just want to be happy!" We seem to believe that "being happy" is life's great quest.

What makes us happy? I can list some things that bring me happiness: a big dinner with all the family gathered round, a hike through the October mountains with blue sky overhead and the brilliant autumn leaves all around, home-made pound cake topped with ice cream, a twenty-inch trout, a six-inch trout. All these things, and so much more, make me happy.

Yet, happiness is fickle, and happiness is fleeting. The common threads of conditions and circumstances determine whether we are happy. Therefore, when circumstances are not conducive—we don't get that raise or promotion, our team doesn't win, it rains on our picnic, our neighbor buys a nicer vehicle than we have—we become **unhappy**.

Someone wisely said: It's not what happens to you, it's what happens in you that matters. JOY is what happens in us! Joy is not a feeling or emotion; rather, it is a **fruit** of the presence of the indwelling Holy Spirit.

The Apostle Paul wrote these words in his letter to the Philippians:

> *In all my prayers for all of you, I always pray with joy . . . and I will continue with all of you for your progress and joy in the faith, so that through my being with you again your joy in Christ Jesus will overflow on account of me . . . Rejoice in the Lord always. I will say it again: REJOICE!* (Philippians 1:4, 25–26; 4:4)

Notice Paul said, "Rejoice in the Lord **always**." Rejoicing is the outward display of the inward joy. Paul wrote these words from prison—PRISON! We wouldn't consider the captivity of prison as favorable circumstances for promoting happiness. Yet, he had JOY! He REJOICED!

Joy, real Christian joy, is not dependent on outward circumstances, but on the inward condition of the heart. When we are yielded to the Holy Spirit and controlled by His presence in our lives, we will have the fruit of joy. We will not be swayed or controlled by the pursuit of the fickle, fleeting feeling of happiness; instead, we will know the forever flowing freedom of joy which cannot be held captive by the circumstances of life. Joy will flow out of us and be seen in our behavior and our faces.

How important is joy to the Christian? Jesus spoke to his disciples the night before his crucifixion. He taught the lesson of the vine and its branches. He taught of the Father's desire for them to bear much fruit. He taught of the necessity of their remaining in his love and obeying his commands. Listen to one of the purposes of his words that night:

> "I have told you this so that **my joy** may be in you and that **your joy** may be complete." (John 15:11)

JOY! HIS JOY! IS IT IN YOU?

YOUR TURN:

(1) Do you have joy because your sins are forgiven and no longer hold you captive?
(2) Do you have joy because Christ is your friend in all circumstances?
(3) Do you have joy because the Father loves you as his own child and is always near?

(4) Do you have joy because you know beyond doubt that there is an eternal home that awaits you?
(5) Please read Galatians 5:22–23.
(6) Pray to be filled with his joy.

Part Fourteen

When The Going Gets Tough

CHAPTER 39

BY DESIGN

But we also rejoice in our sufferings, because we know that suffering produces perseverance; perseverance, character; and character, hope. And hope does not disappoint us, because God has poured out his love into our hearts by the Holy Spirit, whom he has given us.

Romans 5:3–5

It has been a very emotional week for our family. Our twins, Meagan and Brett, graduated from high school. One chapter of their lives has come to an end. Another chapter opens before them.

While trimming the shrubbery this week I came across a cocoon hanging from a limb. We all know from childhood the story of the caterpillar that weaves the cocoon around him, and through the process of metamorphosis becomes a butterfly. It is God's design.

Recently I read an analogy based on the final act of metamorphosis. If you were to attempt (as I did as a child) to help the transformed butterfly out of the cocoon by cutting it open and taking it out, it would die. Even though it has fully developed into a butterfly, it would die.

Why? The story I read explained that the butterfly has to struggle to escape the confines of the cocoon. It has to chew and claw and fight through the tough fibers of its cell. And it is in this **struggle** that it gains the strength necessary to spread its wings in its new state, to fly, and to live. It is God's design.

This process designed into the butterfly can be used as an analogy to apply to us all. But I thought of how it applies to the raising of our children. My children have in so many ways been wrapped and sheltered in a cocoon until now. We've dried their tears and bandaged their skinned knees and always been right beside them. But a time comes when we have to put them in the care of their Creator and trust him in his design for their lives.

We often want our kids to remain in our protective cocoon through the college years. So we pay their way, buy them a vehicle to drive, pick up their credit card bills, and somehow think that they will graduate from college all mature and bold and ready to face the world with strong character. They are turned loose from college just as the falsely freed butterfly.

Sadly, we fail to realize as parents that in our children's mistakes, failures, disappointments, disillusionments, hurts, pains, and heartaches, God is growing them. We fail to realize that it is in the struggle that character is built, and with strong character, maturity.

We need to impress upon our growing children the difficult exhortation of Paul:

"Work out your salvation with fear and trembling . . ." (Philippians 2:12). It is a daily struggle, a daily "working out". We need to help our children realize that the Christian life, therefore, must be a daily surrender of our will to God's: *"For it is God who works in you to will and to act according to his good purpose"* (Philippians 2:13).

I do not pray that my children will have a struggle-free life. Rather, I pray that God will grow them with the strength of Christian character and lead them to maturity in him. That is God's design.

YOUR TURN:

(1) How are you "softening the blows" for your children?
(2) Are you absorbing the consequences of your child's wrong actions?
(3) Does this negating of consequences help them grow?
(4) Does it teach them reality?
(5) Did Christ portray a struggle-free life for the disciples?
(6) Please read Matthew 10:5–42.
(7) Pray that God will give you wisdom in knowing when to let your children know the full weight of the consequences of their actions.

CHAPTER 40

SPRINGER MOUNTAIN

"My burden is light . . ."

Matthew 11:30

While hiking the Appalachian Trail leading to the summit of Grandfather Mountain in North Carolina, I noticed two middle-aged hikers ahead of me. On their backs were packs that looked like those plastic car-top carriers used to transport excess baggage on vacations. The men were plodding wearily up the trail, and I quickly overtook them. As I passed, I couldn't hold my comment. "Those are TREMENOUS packs you guys have!"

One of the men lifted his head and weakly replied, "It's a long way to Maine, ya' know."

There's no way I can say with certainty, but I'm pretty confident in assuming, those two hikers didn't make it to Maine. The load was too much, the burden too encumbering, and the journey too long.

The Appalachian Trail is 2167 miles long. It stretches from Springer Mountain in Georgia to Mt. Katahdin in Maine. Most "through hikers" begin in Georgia in early spring and hike northward to the Maine terminus. Averaging 15 miles of hiking per day, the journey would take about five months. Preparation, discipline, perseverance, and endurance are required to complete the trail from end to end. Packing light is also a mandate.

Leading up to the start point on Springer Mountain is an eight-mile approach trail. Most hikers use that trail to warm up for what lies ahead and to adjust their packs and loads. Many interesting things are found on that approach trail. Iron skillets and pots, axes and hatchets, bulky camp stoves, and other assorted weighty items have been tossed aside. Hikers on Springer Mountain come to a daunting RECKONING: the long, demanding journey ahead will not be made unless the hiker casts off and lays down those burdensome things that will encumber the journey. Only then are they ready to "hit the trail".

All Christians need a "Springer Mountain". The trail begins when we are "born again" and stretches all our remaining days. The journey is long and demanding and requires discipline, perseverance, and endurance. We need to cast off that which weighs us down, lay down the burdens that encumber, and hit the trail focused on the journey set before us.

Many of us bear the unnecessary load of guilt from past sin, and the corresponding weight of shame presses upon us. A moment of reckoning must occur as we accept the freedom that has already been given. Jesus Christ paid the debt that we could not pay. The weight of our past sin has been lifted, and we do not have to carry that burden of guilt and shame. Cast it off, lay it down at the Cross where the debt was paid, and hit the trail set before us.

Many of us bear the unnecessary weight of worldly pursuits. The anxiety of jobs and careers, the obsession over the accumulation of possessions, and the drive toward social recognition and status all contribute to a burdensome load. These are the burdens of a worldly society, and we as Christians too often become encumbered by society's impossible demands. The weight is just too great. We must cast off the soul-draining pursuits of status, lay down our possessions with the realization that we are his stewards, and hit the trail with the balance that comes from putting first the Kingdom of God and His righteousness.

Even the loved ones for whom we feel responsible can be a weight that we cannot carry alone. One of the most difficult times in the life of a parent is the time when a child graduates from high school. Suddenly one chapter of our stewardship is ending. As we watch our child leave for college, our role as a parent becomes unclear to us. The sudden change leaves us feeling out of control. More than anything we want our child to be all right and not to make the mistakes we may have made in our youth. It is often a burden too heavy. But what peace comes when we cast it off to the One who is always watching and caring for our child, lay down the worry as we daily cover our child in prayers, and hit the trail with confidence and faith that our God is able to lead our children on the journey set before them.

As we walk further along the Christian journey, the desire for significance becomes an increasing weight. Does it matter that I am here? Will my life amount to anything? Will I leave anything of real value behind when I am gone? These are questions that arise in our heart and become too burdensome. To believe that our journey is not in vain takes trust in the ways of God. We are given insight into what gives our lives significance in Paul's words:

> *You yourselves are our letter, written on our hearts, known and read by everybody. You show that you are a letter from Christ, the result of our ministry, written not with ink but with the Spirit of the living God, not on tablets of stone but on tablets of human hearts. Such confidence as this is ours through Christ before God. (2 Corinthians 3:2–4)*

We can have confidence in the significance of our journey, because we carry the message that will be written on human hearts. What Christ does through us endures far beyond our personal journey. Our fear of insignificance must be cast off. We must lay down our desire for accolades and hit the trail with full confidence in the purpose Christ sets before us.

Take a moment to consider what Jesus says about our burdens. He realizes that the walk of the disciple cannot be made alone.

> *"Come to me, all you who are weary and burdened, and I will give you rest. Take my yoke upon you and learn from me, for I am gentle and humble in heart, and you will find rest for your souls. For my yoke is easy and my burden is light." (Matthew 11:28–30)*

Jesus says to cast off those weighty burdens we try to carry ourselves, lay it down under his yoke, and hit the trail with a load that is light.

Most hikers who begin the Appalachian Trail do not finish at Mt. Katahdin. Knees are blown out. Ankles are twisted and sprained. The body becomes weaker than the urge to continue. The finish line becomes a point on the trail other than the one originally planned by the hiker.

Similarly, one of the heaviest burdens of our journey is the often suppressed, unspoken uncertainty of the end point. What if the finish is not at the point where we had planned? What if we do not accomplish all that we want to accomplish? What if sickness, injury, or disease cut short our journey? Such questions weigh heavily on our hearts.

Few of us will finish when and where we may envision. Fear of the actual number of our days becomes a burden too much. We need a Springer Mountain for that, as well. Only when we can trust God to number our days according to his plan will we be fully prepared for the journey. We must come to a reckoning that it is not life's duration measured in days, but, rather, life's donation through Christ working in us that matters at the end. We must cast off the anxiety of a finish "too soon", lay down control of the finish point, and hit the trail for the distance God has set.

> *If we live, we live to the Lord; and if we die, we die to the Lord. So, whether we live or die, we belong to the Lord.* (Romans 14:8)

YOUR TURN:

(1) What burdens are too heavy for you?
(2) Will you commit to casting off that which encumbers your Christian walk?
(3) Please read John 15:13–14, and 1 John 3:16.
(4) What does it mean to "lay down your life for a brother"? Does it mean dying for a brother, or living selflessly for others?
(5) Does ownership of self also need a Springer Mountain?
(6) Pray for Christ's yoke to come over you and free you of burden.

CHAPTER 41

ENDURANCE

"Everyone shall hate you because you belong to me. But all of you who endure to the end shall be saved."
Matthew 10:22 (TLB)

One of the most fascinating voyages of exploration ever attempted is chronicled in the book entitled, "South". It is Sir Ernest Shackleton's personal account of a British expedition he led at the outset of World War I. The purposed mission of the expedition was the crossing of the continent of Antarctica. Instead, the ship on which Shackleton and his men were sailing became trapped in the ice surrounding their planned destination.

Shackleton's mission then shifted to attempts to free the ship and its crew and sail to safety. After nine months of futile effort, the ship was crushed by the ice pack and sank to the icy depths. The men were forced to camp on the ice amidst the brutal artic blizzards. Eventually the ice on which they floated began to break apart, which left only one option—taking to the open sea in three small lifeboats.

The tiny boats traversed the turbulent southern seas for 600 miles before beaching on uninhabited Elephant Island. Leaving 22 men on the island, Shackleton took a crew of four and one of the boats in an effort to reach a whaling village on South Georgia Island, 850 miles distant. Miraculously, they found the island, but the winds forced them to land on the opposite side from the village.

Shackleton and two of the four men hiked across the more than twenty miles of uncharted, snow-covered mountain peaks before finally limping into the whaling station. Because another ice pack had enveloped the area, several rescue attempts would be necessary to save the men left on Elephant Island. But Shackleton did not give up until all 26 of his men were safe and on their way back to England.

Into today's lingo this story might be called a great story of "survival". It is, rather, a great story of ENDURANCE. Indeed, the name of the ship on which Shackleton and his men sailed was aptly named the "**Endurance**".

Most of the many gems of wisdom and nuggets of advice given to us upon graduation from high school have been long forgotten (if they were even heard in the first place). However, one statement made by my pastor at the time has remained in my memory: "Don't seek a way out, seek a way through." The statement has been a reminder to me at many of life's junctures.

How often we find ourselves in a critical situation, and the first thing we seek is a way out. Yet, the more I grow in the Christian life, the more I realize the importance of a key character trait in our faith—ENDURANCE!

We only have to read the Scriptures to know its importance. Throughout the Old Testament we are shown God's people facing incredible circumstances that should have caused them to seek a way out. Instead, they stood firm in their faith, trusted God's ways, and endured trials and hardships. We read the accounts of Jesus' disciples and the disciples of the first century church. They faced persecution, prison, and death. Yet, through it all, they endured. They could have fled, but for the sake of the gospel they stood firm in their faith. As we read the history of Christian saints across the centuries, one trait stands out—ENDURANCE!

Today is no different. The call to stand firm and endure has not changed, but we often fail to recognize its importance. When faced with difficulties we are inclined to pray for deliverance, "Lord, just get me out of this mess!" And there are times when the Lord will readily deliver us. More often, however, he calls us to **endure** until a deliverance of his own timing.

In the tenth chapter of Matthew we are given the words of Jesus as he sends out his twelve disciples. His warnings and instructions are clear and specific. He tells them that they are being sent out as sheep among wolves. He warns of the inevitable persecutions and trials. He tells of the hatred they will encounter, but he also assures them of one thing:

> *"Everyone shall hate you because you belong to me. But all of you who **endure** to the end shall be saved." (Matthew 10:22 [TLB])*

Later when Jesus spoke of the end times in the twenty-fourth chapter of Matthew, he echoed that same call:

*"Sin will be rampant everywhere and will cool the love of many. But those **enduring** to the end shall be saved." (Matthew 24:12–13 [TLB])*

Jesus bid his disciples, "endure to the end." His instructions to his disciples have not changed.

How do we, as Christ's disciples today, develop endurance? Is it something for which we pray? Is it some ingredient that is added to our list of character traits? To answer those questions we must understand that endurance is, in a sense, a by-product of something else. That "something else" is PERSEVERANCE. We cannot develop and achieve endurance in our Christian walk without practicing perseverance. Note the word "practicing". Perseverance must become a daily exercise, a daily habit. To know endurance we have to be in the habit of "putting our nose to the grindstone" rather than looking around for the "exit" sign.

In my high school days I played a couple seasons of football. Since I was relatively small (about 130 pounds at the time), my position was running back. During practice the coach would call for sled drills, and my heart would sink. I hated that drill! I thought it was brutal! The coach would stand on the front of a sled shaped liked a saucer, and I would get set in my halfback stance and wait for the signal. The coach would yell; "Go", and the fun began. The object of the drill was to hit the padded bar on the sled with a shoulder, lift up the coach and saucer to a point where only the front end was remaining on the ground, and drive that sled across the field using all the leg and body strength my 130 pounds could muster. The coach would offer "encouraging" words as turf kicked up behind me. "Drive! Drive! Drive! Dig! Dig! Dig!" After what seemed to be 100 yards of driving and digging, he would yell, "Ho!" With heart pounding, legs feeling like rubber, and head throbbing, I would wearily take my place behind the other running backs waiting their turn. A few minutes later the drill would be repeated all over again, and then again.

Why was our coach doing this? Was it to be cruel? Certainly, it was not. He was teaching us to persevere, to keep on driving, to keep on pushing, and not to quit until he gave the call. In the process of persevering, we developed endurance, so that on game day we would be able to run and drive through the line of opponents until the final whistle sounded.

Our Christian walk is no different. Seemingly insurmountable obstacles will be in our path, and we will be called to persevere. James, a brother of Jesus, writes these words to fellow Christians (us):

Consider it pure joy, my brothers, whenever you face trials of many kinds, because you know that the testing of your faith develops perseverance. Perseverance must finish its work so that you may be mature and complete, not lacking anything. (James 1:2–4)

Pure JOY! How many of us consider it pure joy to face trials? Yet, James tells us this is part of the growth process if we are to be complete and mature followers of Christ.

Paul also tells us to have joy when confronted with suffering:

> *But we also rejoice in our sufferings, because we know that suffering produces perseverance; perseverance, character; and character, hope. And hope does not disappoint us, because God has poured out his love into our hearts by the Holy Spirit, whom he has given us. (Romans 5:3–5)*

Our attitude should be one of rejoicing because of what is working within us to build our character. In addition, we have the assurance of hope, which will not disappoint us.

The necessity of perseverance in developing endurance is not only applicable to our trials and suffering; it is also necessary in doing good works in the name of Christ. The radical, rejoicing Paul instructs the Galatians (and us):

> *Let us not become weary in doing good, for at the proper time we will reap a harvest if we do not give up. (Galatians 6:9)*

Take note of the last words of this verse: "IF WE DO NOT GIVE UP." Winston Churchill challenged his countrymen during brutal and relentless attacks by the Nazis, "Never, never, never, never, NEVER—GIVE UP!" And the British people endured.

Doing good can be as trying as trials of persecution and suffering. The tendency is toward weariness. Why should that be the case? Perhaps we are not seeing the rewards that we think we deserve for our service. Or we are not receiving the appreciation we expect, so we grow weary and give up. Jesus said:

> *"No one who puts his hand to the plow and looks back is fit for service in the Kingdom of God." (Luke 9:62)*

When we commit to Christian service—doing good—we cannot look back. We cannot suddenly drop it and quit. If we do so, we are missing the primary element of service, and that is **humility**. Service is often thankless, humiliating work. However, we are assured in God's Kingdom that the humble will be exalted.

The brother in humble circumstances ought to take pride in his high position. (James 1:9)

In the only frame of reference that matters (God's), we should consider humble circumstances of service as a high position. We should rejoice, therefore, in the humility that service brings.

The great desire of our heavenly Father, as told by Jesus in the fifteenth chapter of John, is that we bear much fruit. That is accomplished by persevering in the good works that God has provided us to do.

And we pray this in order that you may live a life worthy of the Lord and may please him in every way: bearing fruit in every good work, growing in the knowledge of God, being strengthened with all power according to his glorious might so that you may have great endurance and patience . . . (Colossians 1:10–11)

The end result of perseverance is **blessedness** and heavenly **reward**. Again listen to the words of James:

*Blessed is the man who perseveres under trial, because when he has stood the test, he will receive the crown of life that God has promised to those who love him. (James 1:12)
As you know, we consider blessed those who have persevered. (James 5:11)*

Consider the Christian progression that leads to spiritual maturity:

Perseverance–Endurance–Fruitfulness–Blessedness–Reward

YOUR TURN:

(1) What is the difference between mere survival and endurance?
(2) Should your prayers be focused more on endurance during trials or on deliverance?
(3) Notice how often the traits of perseverance, endurance, and standing firm are emphasized in the scriptures.
(4) Please read Matthew 5:10–11.
(5) Please read "South" or other accounts of the voyage of the "Endurance".
(6) Pray that God will give you a "no quit" attitude toward his service.

Part Fifteen

Knowing Him

CHAPTER 42

DO YOU WANT TO BREATHE

One thing I ask of the Lord, this is what I seek: that I may dwell in the house of the Lord all the days of my life, to gaze upon the beauty of the Lord and to seek him in his temple.

Psalms 27:4

Close your mouth and press your lips together tightly. Squeeze your nose shut with a thumb and finger. Hold that position for an hour. Can you do it? Or do you want to breathe?

To further illustrate this need, recall your visits to the swimming pool as a child? Without fail, a "pool bully" would be swimming the waters. He would pick on the little kids and hold them (me) under water until they went limp. I soon learned to go limp quickly so that I could surface and breathe again.

The movie "Deliverance" hit the theaters when I was about 20. A friend and I saw the movie and thought a canoe trip down a mountain river would be a swell adventure. Neither of us had done any white-water canoeing, but it certainly didn't look too difficult.

My friend, Steve, purchased a long aluminum canoe (probably best suited for quiet lake expeditions) for the journey. Early one morning we paddled into the current of a mountain river with about 500 pounds of food and camping gear for our two-day odyssey. The first few hours went fairly well, and we handled some challenging white-water runs with ease. Our confidence was building with each conquest.

In the middle of the afternoon we came to a section of the river that split into three channels around a couple of islands. The river also descended rapidly at this point, so the water was white and swift. Back paddling as we surveyed our choices, it was agreed to shoot the far right channel. That run appeared to offer the wildest ride.

We began knifing through the churning, boiling stream taking water in our face as we went. Conditions, however, can change quickly on a stream. Since I was in the front of the canoe, I saw it first—the water seemed to suddenly disappear ahead of us. Yelling back to Steve, I urged him to keep the canoe pointing straight. We were inevitably going over a six to seven-foot drop. For a moment it seemed that we were going to shoot straight over the falls and land safely into a gently flowing pool below. At the lip of the falls, however, a submerged rock caught the front of the canoe, and it careened broadside. In that position we dropped hard into the foam of the falls as water rushed into the canoe. Steve was thrown free on impact, but my legs were trapped under a crossbar as the boat flipped bottom side up. The silver molded metal began floating downstream as I hung underneath.

Oh yeah, I thought I was going to die, but God saved me. The canoe lodged on a rock in the middle of the stream and allowed me to wiggle free. Never will I forget coming up from the water and taking that deep, gasping breath. Did I want to breathe? More than anything else in life at that moment, I wanted to breathe.

How much do we want to know God?

I heard a story about a man who went to St. Augustine with the question, "How can I really know God?" Augustine didn't immediately answer, but instead took him to a local pond. As they waded out into the water, Augustine took the man's head, submerged it into the water and held it there a few seconds (pond bully!). The man came up gasping, but Augustine immediately submerged him again. Pulling him up the second time, Augustine asked, "Do you want to breathe?"

The man exclaimed, "Yes! Of course I want to breathe!"

In his wisdom, St. Augustine then gave the man the answer to his question: "If you want to know God as much as you want to breathe, you will know him."

Jesus' commands always involve our action, and to really know God requires our action. Consider the way Jesus uses the action verb "seek" in these two instances:

> "Seek first his kingdom and his righteousness . . ." (Matthew 6:33)

> "Seek and you will find . . ." (Luke 11:9)

To seek, **really seek**, to know God demands more than a casual groping. It is a lifelong pursuit to know him and his righteousness in our life. Do we really want to know him? Do we want to breathe?

When I was under the canoe floating downstream, I would have given everything I owned just to breathe. What worth would anything have had if I could not take the next breath? When we really want to know God in such a way that no sacrifice is too great, then we are on course to know him.

Listen to one who understood this sacrifice:

> *But whatever was to my profit I now consider loss for the sake of Christ. What is more, I consider everything a loss compared to the surpassing greatness of knowing Christ Jesus my Lord, for whose sake I have lost all things. I consider them rubbish, that I may gain Christ.* (Philippians 3:7–8)

How will we know when we know that we know him? The answer is simple: We will know that we know him when Jesus Christ is manifested in our daily life. When our top priority each day is to know his presence, then we are gaining in our quest.

Do we want to know God as much as we want to breathe? Are we willing to give all, "to count everything a loss compared to the surpassing greatness of knowing Christ Jesus"? When we answer YES to those two questions, I believe we will know him and be found in him.

YOUR TURN:

(1) For further reading on knowing God: *The Pursuit of God*, by A. W. Tozer.
(2) Please read Psalms 34:8. Are you "tasting" the presence of God?
(3) Commit to **devoted** time with the Lord each day.
(4) What is the difference between a "devotional" and "devoted time"?
(5) Pray to know him better today by being aware of his presence.

CHAPTER 43

BIOGRAPHY

And to know this love that surpasses knowledge—that you may be filled to the measure of all the fullness of God.
Ephesians 3:19

The old pine floors creaked and groaned as I made my way down the aisle of musty books. Stopping in front of the section labeled "BIOGRAPHY", I scanned the titles trying to determine whose life I would enter next. As a boy, it was my favorite genre, and I only remember checking out biographies from the 1890's red brick schoolhouse-turned-library. A few of my favorite characters I still recall: Nathan Hale, Abraham Lincoln, Thomas Jefferson, Thomas Edison, Henry Ford, Meriwether Lewis, and Winston Churchill.

The details of these men's lives recorded on the pages of books fascinated me, some enough to read more than once. I learned how many filaments Thomas Edison tried in his light bulb before finding one that would work. I learned how many Model T Fords rolled off the assembly line and all the colors that were offered (black). I really felt as though I knew these men after reading their biography.

Of course, I never really knew any of these men. We never had a relationship as friends, associates or confidants. They were only known from a written record. In fact, most of them lived many years previously and most died long before I was even born. However, I certainly knew all **about** them.

Without a doubt, one of the most popular biographies is found in a collection of four books named after the authors: Matthew, Mark, Luke, and John. We as Christians refer to these four books as the Gospel. These four authors wrote the biography of the author of our faith, Jesus Christ. It is obviously considered required reading for those who want to know about Christ and his ministry on earth. Many have been so fascinated by this man's life that the accounts recorded in those pages have been read and reread many times. Some even consider themselves Gospel scholars and can recite many quotes (passages) of Jesus. A popular speech given by Jesus, such as "The Sermon on the Mount", makes great memorization and recitation material. Knowing all the beatitudes and naming all the disciples also makes a good impression at Sunday school socials.

It is entirely possible to know practically everything **about** Jesus by reading these four books. But we can go much beyond this limited biographical sketch. The books of Prophesy in the in the Old Testament give many characteristics of the Jesus that was to be. The books and letters of the New Testament following the Gospels serve to clarify and expand our knowledge of this man, Jesus.

We may come to the realization, however, that Jesus Christ lived 2000 years ago and died long before we were born. How can we ever know him beyond the written record? Tragically, many Christians believe that a thorough knowledge **about** Jesus is all that is required to live the Christian life. Nothing could be further from Jesus' own desire for us. He wants a RELATIONSHIP—a personal relationship.

All knowledge about Jesus is certainly important for the Christian's growth, and study of the scriptures should be a daily habit. Many times in the letters of the Apostles we are told to increase our knowledge of Christ. However, if we desire to follow him as a disciple, a more intimate relationship is essential.

How can we have a relationship with one who lived and died 2000 years ago? Simply, we must come to realize a central truth. He is not just a man of history; rather, he is the central theme of history. He died, but he is risen, and he lives—**today**. And since he lives, we can have a relationship with him. We must quit thinking from a strictly human, natural, and worldly perspective if we are to know him—really KNOW him.

With the new life that we have been given, the ability to have a personal relationship with our Savior and Lord has also been given. Notice the word "ability". The words "opportunity" and "privilege" may also be used in describing Jesus' desire for a personal relationship with his disciples. Since it is such a privilege, why do we not seize the opportunity? An answer to this question may be ascertained from a story found in Luke 10:

> As Jesus and his disciples were on their way, he came to a village where a woman named Martha opened her home to him. She had a sister called Mary, who sat at the Lord's feet listening to what he said. But Martha was distracted by all the preparations that had to be made. She came to him and asked, "Lord, don't you care that my sister has left me to do the work by myself? Tell her to help me!"
>
> "Martha, Martha," the Lord answered, "you are worried and upset about many things, but only one thing is needed. Mary has chosen what is better, and it will not be taken away from her." (Luke 10:38–40)

Of the lessons that can be learned from this story, some are the primary ingredients to having a relationship with the same Lord. Can you see how Mary considered it a privilege to be in the Lord's presence? Can you see how she did not squander the opportunity?

To have a personal relationship with Jesus, we can learn these simple lessons from Mary's devotion. Sit at the Lord's feet and listen to what he is saying. He tells us it is the only thing that is needed. It is the better way, and in this better way we know the person of Jesus Christ as he moves in us and through us. It is not just knowing **about** him that matters. It is **knowing him personally** as Lord and Savior.

YOUR TURN:

(1) Answer honestly—Do you really know him?

(2) Please read the words from the hymn, "In the Garden". Does this speak of a personal relationship?
(3) Will you commit this week to devoted time in order to know him more?
(4) Pray with the desire to really know him and be found in him.

CHAPTER 44

THE WHISPER OF THE HEART

We have not received the spirit of the world but the Spirit who is from God, that we may understand what God has freely given us.

1 Corinthians 2:12

The story is told of a man named Clyde who moved to the hills of North Georgia. He began to take an interest in one of the local activities, coon hunting. The men he met would boast about the number of coons treed on a given night, but mostly they would brag about their dogs. Those coon dogs brought them more joy, it seemed, than their own families.

Clyde began inquiring about where he, too, could get one of those prized coon dogs. Everyone told him to see a man named Lucas, so he got directions to his farm and went to visit.

Lucas was more than happy to show off his dogs and was especially proud of a dog named Redleg. Clyde wanted to know what made Redleg so special. Lucas called the dog over and told him to sit. He then picked up a short length of 2x4 board and whacked Redleg over the head. "Redleg, fetch my hunting boots." The dog ran to the front porch, picked up the boots beside the rocking chair, ran back and dropped them at the man's feet. Lucas again ordered the dog to sit, whacked him over the head, and gave another command, "Redleg, open the barn door." Redleg ran to the barn, grabbed a rope on the door by his teeth, and pulled the door open.

Clyde was very impressed with the intelligence of Redleg but was equally confused by the techniques of Lucas. He expressed his confusion, "That's quite a dog, but I don't understand why you punish your dog before you even tell him what to do."

"Punish him?" Lucas was incredulous. "I'm just getting his attention!" (Those with teenage boys will understand the implications to this story).

How often the circumstances of our life whack us like a board to the head. Sometimes it takes something drastic to get our attention, and God can use such circumstances to speak to us. God more often speaks to us, however, in a very different way—in a "still, small voice" (1 Kings 19:12).

The Holy Spirit is that voice of God that speaks to us not in a shout, but in a whisper. If we are not listening, we will not hear what He has to tell us. If we are not tuned to the same frequency, we will miss hearing Him as well.

We may claim to want to know the Holy Spirit's leading about a matter. Yet, we make so much noise beating our own drum that we cannot hear the Spirit's voice, so we conclude that God is silent. Or we are living in such a way that the whisper is squelched by our own actions.

I've wondered many times why God doesn't use a bullhorn or flash neon signs to overcome these obstacles that we put in the way—and show us his way. I believe the reason is simply that God wants us to "be still, and know" (Psalms 46:10), and in that holy silence we hear the Spirit's whisper.

Hearing alone, however, is not enough. Yielding must follow hearing, and in that yielding we are given clarity and direction. Then we find each aspect of our life yielding to the voice and control of the Holy Spirit; from our prayer life to our work life, from our home life to our social life—all comes under the control of that whisper of the heart.

So I say, live by the Spirit, and you will not gratify the desires of the sinful nature . . . Since we live by the Spirit, let us keep in step with the Spirit. (Galatians 5:16, 25)

LISTEN–HEAR–YIELD–FOLLOW

YOUR TURN:

(1) Please read 1 Kings 19:11–13. Was the Lord trying to get Elijah's attention before he spoke in a "gentle whisper"?
(2) Take 10 minutes now to be still and listen for the gentle whisper of God's Holy Spirit.

(3) Please read Galatians 5:16–26.
(4) Pray that you will be tuned to the whisper of his voice.

Part Sixteen

What's Left

CHAPTER 45

ALL THE INGREDIENTS

And now these three remain: faith, hope, and love. But the greatest of these is love.

1 Corinthians 13:13

Friday nights have become "chili night" at the Bond house. This has been a selfish victory for me since I'm the biggest chili connoisseur of the family. For now, at least, Friday chili night is an infant-stage tradition.

On a recent Friday evening, I arrived home from work to find Jill standing over the stove cutting up all the peppers, onions, mushrooms and other ingredients necessary to carry on the tradition. After cooking and simmering for about an hour, the chili was ready for my culinary delight—I thought.

After slicing some cheese to place on top and grabbing a few crackers, I sat down and dug in. It is my firm belief that chili is only chili if the hair on the back of my neck is soaking wet and my sinuses are completely cleared within the first five bites. Nothing like that happened. Obviously, something was missing.

"Honey, did you remember to put in the spices?" I asked.

Her eyes got big. She didn't even have to answer. The other ingredients were there: beans, meat, peppers, onions, tomato sauce, and mushrooms. Missing were the spices that make chili, chili. **Without the spices, it's just bean soup!**

When we look at the body of believers, we discover a variety of "ingredients" that we consider the spiritual gifts. The Bible speaks, in 1 Corinthians 12, of these different ingredients and how they combine to form the whole. The apostle Paul then speaks of the "greater gifts" and the "most excellent way". What is the "greater" and "most excellent" ingredient required in the body of believers? God uses Paul's writings to lead us to that missing ingredient which makes all the difference. It is found in the thirteenth chapter of First Corinthians.

Suppose I am gifted in **speaking** the languages of all people and even of angels, yet lack that one ingredient? Then I am only a "resounding gong or a clanging cymbal". Suppose I have the gift of **prophecy** and can **fathom** all **mysteries** and all **knowledge**. Suppose I also have the **faith** that can move mountains, but am missing that one ingredient, then I am "nothing". Suppose I further **give** all my **possessions** to the poor and **martyr** my **body** to the flames, but have forgotten the one thing, then I gain nothing.

We are told the qualities of this key ingredient in the same chapter. It is patient, kind, not envious, not boastful or proud, not rude, not self-seeking, not easily angered or a record keeper of wrongs. It does not delight in evil but rejoices in truth. It protects, trusts, hopes, and perseveres. **It never fails.**

Most of us know that key ingredient, that one thing that makes all the difference in the life of a Christian. It is LOVE. Without it, all our efforts, all our service, all our talents, all our gifts are in vain. All-encompassing love is THE INGREDIENT that turns a bland Christian into a vibrant Christian. And love must permeate all aspects of our life if we are to be effective in our service to Christ.

Jesus was asked to give the greatest commandment. The two-part command centered on that one essential ingredient:

Jesus replied: "Love the Lord your God with all your heart and with all your soul and with all your mind. This is the first and greatest commandment. And the second is like it: Love your neighbor as yourself." (Matthew 22:37–39)

One command—two parts—LOVE GOD AND LOVE OTHERS. We cannot look at the life of our Lord without realizing that love defines his mission and permeates who he is.

The disciple John writes in his first letter:

Dear friends, let us love one another, for love comes from God. Everyone who loves has been born of God and knows God.

God is love. Whoever lives in love lives in God, and God in him. In this way, love is made complete among us so that we will have confidence on the day of judgment, because in this world we are like him. (1 John 4:7, 16–18)

Godly love is THE INGREDIENT and we are the vessel into which it is added. Love must blend and mix with our whole being—our words, actions and thoughts—and we are known to be his by its presence. Without it we are nothing. With it we are complete, and WE ARE LIKE HIM.

YOUR TURN:

(1) Please read 1 Corinthians 13.
(2) Are you displaying the qualities of the key ingredient?
(3) Do you often perform Christian service with the attitude of obligation rather than with the attitude of love?
(4) Please read 1 John 4.
(5) Pray that love will be your aim.

CHAPTER 46

I WAS HERE

This is the disciple who testifies to these things and who wrote them down. We know that his testimony is true.
John 21:24

While climbing over a large boulder in a mountain stream, the boldly carved inscription across the top caught my attention. Etched into the stone in letters four or five inches high was the name, "DONNIE MOON II". Donnie II had made a considerable effort in this iron-hard granite to display his name.

Why did he make such an effort? Was he claiming ownership of that particular chunk of granite? No. Donnie II was making a statement: I WAS HERE!

Running deep within us all is the need to somehow let the world know, "I was here!" I've seen other rocks along streams with inscriptions, some made by early nineteenth-century explorers. More often we see carvings in the trunks of trees, especially beech trees, letting us know by initials or full name, "Hey, I was here!" Look at any old wooden school desk (made when boys could carry pocket knives), and this desire for recognition is evident with many names and initials.

Many of us choose to make the announcement in a much more sophisticated manner. Perhaps we dream of monuments, buildings, highways, bridges, or parks built in our honor and bearing our name. All this is done because we want others to know, "I was here!"

The word describing this need is **legacy**. It represents what we leave behind when we are gone. Most of us will think little of our legacy until we reach our 40's, and we begin realizing our mortality. Many times we choose superficial symbols as a legacy and make them our goal.

What will be the Christian's legacy? What will we leave behind? Our legacy is OUR TESTIMONY. Our testimony is the record of God's work in our life. Not only is it a record of past events, but it is also a record of how God is working each day. Our testimony is a **book** in progress with a new page written each day.

The Apostle Paul told the Corinthians:

> *You yourselves are our letter, written on our hearts, known and read by everybody. You show that you are a letter from Christ, the result of our ministry, written not with ink but with the Spirit of the living God, not on tablets of stone but on tablets of human hearts.* (2 Corinthians 3:2–3)

That puts it in perspective. Our testimony is a **letter** from Christ, written on human hearts. What should our letter read? Listen to John's answer:

Anyone who believes in the Son of God has this testimony in his heart . . . And this is the testimony: God has given us eternal life, and this life is in his Son. (1 John 5:10a, 11)

Our testimony is also a **walk**. We follow a path, a course of action and behavior, and in that walk our testimony is manifested. The walk is not of a trailblazer, but of a follower. The walk is patterned after whom we follow.

This is how we know we are in him: Whoever claims to live in him must walk as Jesus did. (1 John 2:5b, 6)

I urge you to live a life worthy of the calling you have received. (Ephesians 4:1)

Since our testimony is seen in our walk, we must take great care not to cause others to stumble. Paul was keenly aware of this in his ministry:

We put no stumbling block in anyone's path so that our ministry will not be discredited. (2 Corinthians 6:3)

The phrase "lose our testimony" is often repeated among Christians, and refers to our testimonial walk. We cannot, of course, lose our salvation, but we can stray in our walk outside of God's will and, hence, lose the effectiveness of our testimony. Such straying is, in itself, a stumbling block to others who may be observing our walk, and "Christ in us" becomes obscured.

What is the significance of our "letter from Christ" and our "walk" with Christ? Simply put, there is great **power** in our testimony. True testimony carries the power of the Spirit of God, and listeners and seekers can realize its sincerity and genuineness. The Bible provides many examples of this. One such example is found in the fifth chapter of Mark:

> *A man with an evil spirit who lived in the tombs came up to Jesus. Here was a man who everyone had written off as doomed. Their attempts to chain him had failed. No one could subdue him. But Jesus cast out the spirit of evil, and the man was healed. The once demon-possessed man begged to go with Jesus, but Jesus instructed him:*
> *"Go home to your family and tell them how much the Lord has done for you, and how he has had mercy on you." So the man went away and began to tell in the Decapolis how much Jesus had done for him.* **And all the people were amazed.** *(Mark 5:19–20)*

Another powerful example is found in a Samaritan woman's testimony recorded in the fourth chapter of John:

> *The woman said, "I know that Messiah (called Christ) is coming. When he comes, he will explain everything to us." Then Jesus declared, "I who speak to you am he."*
> *Then, leaving her water jar, the woman went back to the town and said to the people,* **"Come, see a man** *who told me everything I ever did. Could this be the Christ?" They came out of the town and made their way toward him.*
> *Many of the Samaritans from that town* **believed** *in him* **because of the woman's testimony,** *"He told me everything I ever did." So when the Samaritans came to him, they urged him to stay with them, and he stayed two days. And* **because of his words** *many more became believers.*

> *They said to the woman, "We no longer believe just because of what you said; now we have heard for ourselves, and we know that this man really is the Savior of the world. (John 4:25–26, 28–30, 39–42)*

What a story of the power of testimony! Take note of the progression. The woman met Jesus and believed him to be the Christ, went to the town to tell others (her question, "Could this be the Christ?" was actually a proclamation, "This must be the Christ!"), led them all to meet Jesus, and, hearing him, they also believed. The Samaritan townspeople believed both because of the woman's testimony and because of their meeting and hearing the Savior. It was Christ who saved. It was the woman's testimony that led others to him.

Such is the power of our testimony. It is not who we are—it is what Christ has done in us. Indeed, it is CHRIST IN US!

> *I have been crucified with Christ and I no longer live, but Christ lives in me. (Galatians 2:20)*

Therein lies the power of our testimony.

The **purpose** of our testimony should have one aim: to lead others to meet Christ and find salvation through him. After Paul's testimony before King Agrippa, that purpose was clearly stated:

> *Then Agrippa said to Paul, "Do you think that in such a short time you can persuade me to be a Christian?" Paul replied, "Short time or long—I pray God that not only you but all who are listening to me today may become what I am, except for these chains." (Acts 26:28–29)*

What will remain when we are gone? What will say, "I was here"? Let us not seek a legacy written on monuments or buildings. Even the stone that marks our grave will fade and crumble with time. Let us, instead, leave an eternal inscription written on the hearts and lives of those we touch and lead to meet this Jesus.

All that will matter in the end, and all that will remain is who we are in Christ.

YOUR TURN:

(1) Please read Acts 26, 1 John 5, and 2 Corinthians 6.
(2) Have you "lost your testimony" because your walk has strayed?
(3) Is the testimonial page you are presently writing going to lead anyone to meet Jesus?
(4) What will remain when you are gone?
(5) Pray that God will show you the "big picture" of why you are here.

Part Seventeen

Relationships

CHAPTER 47

RELATED BY BLOOD

However, do not rejoice that the spirits submit to you, but rejoice that your names are written in heaven.
Luke 10:20

In relation to academic and career interests, my two sisters and I have little in common. Even though we grew up together in the same home environment, our adult pursuits have taken different directions.

My older sister has a graduate degree in library science. She has been employed in the state university library system for over twenty-five years. Don't get me wrong, I've done my time in the library, and I enjoy reading. But spending most of my waking hours in a library isn't my idea of fun.

My younger sister also has an exciting graduate degree—medieval literature. When we get together now, the last subject I wish to discuss is the writing of Chaucer.

Yet, they are my sisters, and I am their brother. I love them, and they love me. After all, we're related by blood. But they are different in personality and created for different purposes.

In the family of God there are many dissimilarities among believers. We may not share the same interests, hobbies, clothing styles, politics, skin colors, languages, or appetites. Yet, that which binds us together should be greater by far than any of our many differences.

My older sister has another interest—genealogy. She has spent hundreds of hours researching and tracing the lineage of both our mother's and our father's families. Some interesting discoveries have been made, including one famous cousin. My maternal great, great, . . . (I forget the exact number of "greats") grandfather was hung as a Tory during the Revolutionary War. The counterpart fraternal grandfather fought on the other side in the Revolutionary Army.

The genealogies have been organized and recorded in large notebooks with page after page of names and our relationship to each one listed. I'm sure that among all those ancestors many diverse interests and personalities are represented. Yet, we're all related by blood.

Many different interests and personalities are represented by Christians. Often we may think we have little in common with another believer, but we are all brothers and sisters in Christ. We should love one another regardless of the differences that simply do not matter. Be aware that Satan will use these differences to try to pull us apart.

As brothers and sisters in a sacred genealogy, our names also are written in a book—the Lamb's Book of Life. And all whose names are written there are related by blood—THE BLOOD OF JESUS CHRIST.

YOUR TURN:

(1) Notice the many times the writers in the New Testament use the term "brothers".
(2) Whether you use the term or not, do you think of such a relationship existing among believers?
(3) What brotherly or sisterly service can you perform today?
(4) Pray for a deeper awareness of the relationship that exists between you and fellow believers.

CHAPTER 48

FATHER'S DAY

Fathers, do not exasperate your children; instead, bring them up in the training and instruction of the Lord.
Ephesians 6:4

This is our day, fathers. It is a day set aside to honor how great we are. Many of us read those cards we've been given and get pretty "puffed up". Our children hug us, adore us, and make us feel so proud of ourselves.

Think back to the time when you first took on the title of FATHER. For me, it was November 9, 1982. Within the space of a few minutes I became a father twice with the birth of our twins. The overwhelming fear I expressed at that time was, "Am I ready for this?"

Do we, however, remember our actual roles in becoming a father? Our wives will remind us that it was they who had the hard part and who did all the work. For eight or nine months they saw their bodies change shape as they adjusted for the extra baggage. They will also tell us that childbirth is not the most pleasant or painless experience in life. If we're really honest with ourselves, fathers, we'll admit that our part in becoming a father was very minimal—and certainly not painful.

So why are we "puffed up"?

My children gave me cards today—hand-made cards, the best kind. When I read their cards it gave me an attitude not of pride, but of humility. How could God have blessed me so richly?

Father's Day should be one of our reflection days when we pause to consider what it means to be a father. As Christians, it needs to be a day of recognizing our responsibilities as Godly fathers, as well. The one word that sums up our responsibilities as Godly fathers is STEWARDSHIP. We are to be good stewards of God's gifts, and our children are one of his greatest earthly gifts to us.

Let me make just four points to aid in our stewardship:

(1) Enter and continue into fatherhood with an attitude of THANKFULNESS. Realize that our children are a precious gift of God's creation. They are the unique work of his hands. Express that thankfulness each day.
(2) Among the lessons we teach our children, teach them "THE LAW OF SOWING AND REAPING". Let them learn and know that there are consequences for their choices, and that their life will be the sum of all their choices. We tend, as parents, to want to shelter and to soften the blow of our child's wrong

actions. Instead, we should mostly allow them to face the consequences of wrong choices, however difficult that may be for them and for us. If they do not learn it in childhood, it will be a more painful lesson to learn in adulthood. On the positive side of that lesson, we should teach that to have a fruitful harvest, they must sow good seeds. That, also, should be a daily lesson evidenced by our life.

(3) LOVE YOUR WIFE. This gives great security for them in a society of broken marriages and homes, and it gives them a solid foundation on which to build their own marriage in the future. Our children should see us express our love in words and deeds so that there will be no doubt—Dad loves Mom. This, also, must be seen each day.

(4) We must BE THE SPIRITUAL LEADER OF OUR FAMILY. In order to be the leader, we must, ourselves, have a right relationship with God. That must always be settled first.

My own father gave me many things. One of the most treasured is a little New Testament I received as a child. On the inside cover, written by my father's hand, are the steps to salvation and the scriptural references. No lesson we ever teach is more important or more lasting than leading them, by example and through God's Word, to a personal relationship with Jesus Christ.

Our children will look for a role model. If we are to be that model for them and if we are to be an example of a Godly father, then we must follow the example given us by our heavenly Father. God is our example of Father. HE IS FATHER.

YOUR TURN:

(1) What do your children most desire from you as their father?
(2) What do you consider your primary role as a Christian father?
(3) Tell your children how special they are—today.
(4) Consider this statement: "It's not what we bought them, it's what we taught them that will matter."
(5) Pray for wisdom and guidance in being a Godly father.

CHAPTER 49

MOTHER'S DAY

And you, my child, will be called a prophet of the Most High; for you will go on before the Lord to prepare the way for him, to give his people the knowledge of salvation through the forgiveness of their sins.

Luke 1:76–77

Take a moment to think back, mothers. It's nearing the end of your pregnancy. Suddenly you see all the things that need to be done around the home. You clean every corner, scrub every surface, organize, and straighten from top to bottom. What is this phenomenon of urgency called? NESTING!

My first experience with this odd behavior was during my wife's first pregnancy. She educated me on the process. Of course, the term is derived by what we see birds do in the spring. They prepare the nest for the young ones soon to come.

Moms, you prepare the nest for the child to come into the world. That is part of your job. What is an even more important job for the Godly mom, however, is preparing the heart of the child for God.

Of all the earthly jobs of a mom, what could be more important than preparing the future home of their child's Creator. The job involves both a preparation to receive the Holy Spirit and a preparation to serve as His dwelling place. Only through a total commitment is this preparation achieved.

Let there be no misunderstanding, the mom cannot put the Holy Spirit in their child's heart. The mom cannot force Jesus Christ to enter. The mom cannot make a child love God. Does that diminish the importance of the Godly mom's role?

To answer that question, let's look at the opposite example. Let's look at an ungodly mom. When I see the home environment and the example set by some moms, I can only think of an analogy in baseball. Those children are starting life with an 0–2 count. When a batter faces a count of no balls and two strikes, his chances of getting a hit and reaching base are diminished considerably. It doesn't mean he doesn't have a chance, but it means his chances are slim.

This situation relates to the child who is raised in a home where the mom has no personal commitment to God. No preparation for the child's receiving the witness of the Holy Spirit is made. No foundation for a Godly life is laid.

Godly moms, never discount your importance or your role in making that preparation in the heart of your child. Only God knows where I would be today had not my mom prepared my heart to receive Christ at an early age. It was that foundation that kept me from sinking during years of rebellion. It was her prayers that helped bring me back from a distant land. Furthermore, when I witness my own children's walk with the Lord, I am made aware of Jill's commitment to preparing their hearts for his Spirit.

YOUR TURN:

(1) Think of the ways your own mom prepared your heart for God.
(2) If you did not have a Godly mom, who influenced you in a Godly way?
(3) Pray for wisdom in preparing your child's heart for receiving the Holy Spirit.
(4) Will you make or renew a commitment right now to "prepare the way of the Lord" in your child?

CHAPTER 50

CHARLIE

Let us therefore make every effort to do what leads to peace and to mutual edification.

Romans 14:19

The labor union had made the call to strike. Informed by labor negotiators that contract talks had broken down, more than 200,000 workers were idled with the announcement. Of the many workers idled, I was one. My view of the strike call differed from most of my co-workers. I believed a power play to strengthen the hand of the union was being made at the expense of the workers represented.

Living in a "right to work" state, however, I had a choice. The decision was simple: honor the strike and stay out of work until the union directed otherwise, or cross the picket line and work during the strike. My hopes were to avoid having to make that decision, and I waited the first three or four days thinking the strike would be short-lived. When it was obvious at that point that the labor stoppage could continue for a while, I decided to cross over and work for the company that hired me to work. It seemed the right thing to do.

The night before going back to work was spent making phone calls to co-workers with whom I could share my decision and my reasons for the decision. They understood and respected what I was about to do. A couple of co-workers were also crossing over the next morning to work. It was one of the most gut-wrenching decisions of my life, because I realized that those who honored the strike believed that they were making the right decision, as well. Much of my reasoning was based on the way I was raised. My parents always taught me to give 100% to my employer. I was compensated by an agreed-upon amount for my efforts, and my responsibility was to be a loyal worker until that agreement between the two of us ceased. It was my belief the agreement still applied. My loyalty extended further to my customers. They depended on my service and, in reality, wrote my paycheck.

As I said, not everyone saw it the same way. Driving through the picket line each day was beyond stressful—it was anguish! Co-workers, with whom I had tried to develop not only working relationships, but also friendships, were suddenly calling me "SCAB" (along with a few descriptive adjectives). One of those who participated in the name-calling was a co-worker and union steward by the name of Charlie.

Although the experience hurt, I grew closer to God during this period. My pleas for strength were constant. God granted me endurance during the barbed-word attacks. Usually I would look straight ahead during the verbal assaults and not show any emotion. But it still hurt.

Eventually the strike ended. Everyone went back to work, but to say that everything returned to normal would not be accurate in any way. Those of us who chose to dishonor union instructions were ostracized in a concerted effort to make working conditions miserable. The primary weapon was the silent treatment, as though we didn't exist. Our presence was not acknowledged, and requests for assistance were ignored. One of those who no longer spoke to me was Charlie.

This change in our relationship was especially hurtful, since I had known Charlie for several years. He had served me as his customer before I became a co-worker. Did I respond to this treatment in a Christian way? If the response "two can play this game" is the Christian response, then give me a gold cross. I played that game well for the next four years. Charlie and I did not speak to one another during that entire time.

As someone whose witness and testimony for the Lord was supposed to be a priority, I managed to compartmentalize this grudge. Yet, I knew that I was wrong in my behavior.

Many mornings I would arrive early to work and park my vehicle so that I could watch the sunrise as I had my quiet time of prayer and Bible study. I would often see Charlie arrive and walk across the parking lot. God began to deal with me. He began to convict me of the wrong way I was behaving. My prayers became prayers for forgiveness and restoration so that I would be the witness I needed to be. God gave me the ability to understand Charlie's point of view and to forgive any wrong I thought had been done to me. I prayed for a way to make things right and to seek reconciliation as an ambassador for Christ.

I knew I had to make a move to end the stalemate. Yet, it wasn't I who made the first move. GOD MOVED.

A group of us as Christians had begun a prayer circle that met each morning before starting work. One morning we had a new member join our circle—Charlie. Without any doubt, God was answering my prayer and putting before me the opportunity that I sought. With the grace that only God gives, I reached out my hand and said to Charlie, "Forgive me. I have shunned you for years because of what happened during the strike. I was wrong. I want to be your friend, but more than anything else, I want to be your brother in Christ."

Charlie responded, "It's not a problem." Years of bitterness were washed away in an instant. The power of forgiveness is so great! God had worked to restore, and over the next few months he would work to build a new relationship. You see, Charlie had met Jesus Christ and had dedicated his life to being one of his disciples. He became a powerful witness of God's grace, both at the workplace and in the field in front of his customers.

Several months later I resigned from my job. My wife and I were changing directions in our life and seeking new opportunities for God to use us. We would be moving from Georgia to the mountains of East Tennessee.

The men of the prayer circle honored me with a "going away" breakfast. We read from the Bible certain verses that had been a source of power and vision in our lives. Each of the men spoke of certain memories, but mostly we spoke of how God had used us and how he would continue to use us wherever we were. Charlie was sitting across the table from me. Looking me in the eyes, he spoke these words that I will never forget: "Gary, when I first met you I called you my customer. Then I called you a co-worker. Then I called you names. Now I call you my BROTHER."

Indeed, Charlie and I are brothers. Through the awesome power of forgiveness and God's amazing grace, we are forever—**BROTHERS**.

YOUR TURN:

(1) Please read Matthew 5:9.
(2) Please read James 3:18.
(3) Is there someone with whom you need to make peace?
(4) Will you commit to that peace making?
(5) Pray for God to open a door for you to be a peacemaker.

CHAPTER 51

PARTNERS

For we are God's fellow workers; you are God's field, God's building.

1 Corinthians 3:9

Howdy, podner. So goes the old cowboy greeting we heard in TV westerns. Occasionally we still hear "partner" used as a replacement for buddy, pal, friend, or dude. Some of us call our spouse a partner, and so we should. Others may have a business partnership, which might seem as binding as a marriage.

Those of us who have experienced business partnerships can tell of varying experiences. In ideal situations, one partner compliments the other. In areas where one may be weak, the other partner lends strength, and the business is made stronger than either of the partners operating alone.

On the other hand, some business owners encounter partners that aren't at all what they envisioned when the partnership began. Some partners lack pure motives and may be looking out for their own exclusive interests, rather than the interests of the other partner or the business. Some partners may be just plain dishonest and, as a result, cannot be trusted. Some partners may take from the business far more than they give in return. Some partners are not dependable and may at times not even "show up".

How would it be to have a partner who always wants the best for us, never gives us bad advice, always out gives us, is always available and on the job 24 hours a day and seven days a week? God is that kind of partner.

A book I recently read chronicled the life of a man who partnered with God in business. The autobiography was titled: "R. G. LeTourneau: Mover of Men and Mountains".

Mr. LeTourneau found his calling in life as a businessman—not just any businessman, however, but as God's businessman. LeTourneau considered himself simply a mechanic that God used. He built, with God as his partner, a giant international company that manufactured earth-moving equipment. Most of these brute machines were LeTourneau's own design, and he loved the challenge of making ever-larger machines that could scrape and dig, lift and haul, and simply move earth in mammoth quantities from one place to another.

God blessed R. G. LeTourneau, because he was the example of a good steward. LeTourneau took what God had given him and, with God as his partner, multiplied it many times.

LeTourneau's account of the acceptance of his calling and the beginning of his partnership with God should be required reading for all Christian businesspeople:

"All right, if that is what God wants me to be, I'll try to be His businessman. By the time I started up the tractor to begin the day's work, all my doubts were gone. If I didn't amount to much, I felt, it was because I had tried to struggle along too much on my own. Now that I was in business to serve God, in a sort of partnership, as it were, how could I fail?"

"I would not lightly refer to God as my partner. He is my Lord and Savior, and I am His servant. But by His grace He has made us members of His family, and we can refer to him as our Father which art in Heaven. More than that, He has let us be 'workers, together with Him'. The Bible says, 'We then, as workers, together with Him, beseech you also that ye receive not the grace of God in vain' (2 Corinthians 6:1). So it is in that sense that I mean we are partners, remembering always that real partners don't try to see how much one can get from the other. They work for the good of the partnership. They try to help each other." [1]

R. G. LeTourneau died June 1, 1969, in his eighty-first year, but his legacy and the fruits of his partnership with God live on. The overseas ministries begun during business ventures are still touching lives. LeTourneau College in Texas, founded in 1946, continues as a four-year institute of technology. Toccoa Falls College in Toccoa, Georgia, is a Christian college that LeTourneau supported

---

[1] LeTourneau, *R.G. LeTourneau: Mover of Men and Mountains* (Chicago: Moody Press, 1972), 110

financially at a critical time in its history. Lake Louise Conference Center and campground outside of Toccoa was built by LeTourneau and is now a Baptist assembly facility.

Although I never met or knew Mr. LeTourneau, I have many connections with him. My mother worked in LeTourneau's earth-moving equipment plant in Toccoa during World War II and remembers his visits. I lived as a preschooler in the shadow of that Toccoa plant and played with a model of one of his inventions, the Tournapull, in the dirt of our back yard. My first memories of fishing were from a rock by the shore of Lake Louise. My daughter, Meagan, attended a semester at Toccoa Falls College.

The story of R. G. LeTourneau's life touched my life and blessed me. More than three decades after his death, lives are being touched for Jesus Christ because R. G. LeTourneau made a partnership with God in his business.

Whether it is raising our children and managing the home, presiding over an international company, or cooking french fries at a fast food restaurant, we all have a business. We all need to know that God wants to be our partner. Understand, however, the kind of partnership he desires. God cannot be a silent partner, where we expect all his resources and blessings, but ask him to stay out of the day-to-day operations. God will not accept a 50% - 50% partnership, where we choose which half of the business falls under God's control. Rather, God's plan requires a 100% - 100% partnership. When we honor him and commit 100% of ourselves to him, he will honor our business with 100% of himself.

RELATIONSHIPS

Our partnership with God is not formed by a binding legal contract. It is formed and bound by the Covenant of his Word.

I can do everything through him who gives me strength. (Philippians 4:13)

YOUR TURN:

(1) What does it mean to be "co-laborers" with God?
(2) Please read 1 Corinthians 15:58.
(3) Do you trust God enough to make him your business partner?
(4) Can you see how stewardship and a partnership with God go hand in hand?
(5) Pray that God will lead you into a partnership.

CHAPTER 52

SONSHIP

Because those who are led by the Spirit of God are sons of God. For you did not receive a spirit that makes you a slave again to fear, but you received the Spirit of sonship. And by him we cry, "Abba, Father."
Romans 8:14–15

My friend, Gregg, had taken a voluntary separation from a company where he had worked as an engineer for thirteen years. He and I were meeting weekly at the time for breakfast and a time of sharing and accountability. Gregg used this period of unemployment to catch his breath and prayerfully consider the course for the second part of his life. In effect, it was his "halftime".

During one of our breakfast meetings, he brought the outline of a well-conceived concept for a service business. Since Gregg was a capable handy man and had done much of the construction in his own house, he believed himself capable of satisfying a need that existed for a trusted handy man for the elderly. His marketing plan was based on the idea of "sonship", in the sense that he would be doing the work as conscientiously as would the customer's own son.

A few trial balloons were floated with senior citizen groups, but none returned. It had certainly seemed on paper like a good business idea. Gregg eventually took another engineering job and launched into his second half, and his idea for "sonship" faded.

God works in mysterious and wonderful ways. Gregg didn't conceive the name "sonship" for his business. He unknowingly gave me the name for the new business and accompanying ministry to which God was leading me. Coming out of our own "halftime", Jill and I were in the initial stages of preparing for the change of location and direction. Jill had sold her clothing business, and I had enrolled in auctioneer school. We were getting our house in Athens, Georgia ready to sell, and I would be leaving my job of thirteen years. At the end of our daughter's school year, June 2002, we hoped to be living in the mountains of East Tennessee.

Different names had been considered for this new venture and "tent-maker" ministry, but none seemed exactly right. What would it be named? Do I even need to tell you? "**SONSHIP**", of course. No other name could better exemplify the relationship that I have grown to know so well and that I want to share.

As often as we talk of having a personal relationship with God and with Jesus Christ, do we stop to consider the nature of that "relation"? Let me attempt to answer in a personal way what the relation is, and what it means to me.

When, as a boy of eight, I walked down the aisle of a small Baptist church and expressed the desire to make Christ my savior, a relationship began. At the time, I did not fully understand all the meaning of that relationship. I was an infant, a new believer, and a babe in Christ. Yet, in that profession of faith I became part of the family of God, which meant that I became a brother to Christ and one of God's sons.

You are all sons of God through faith in Christ Jesus. (Galatians 3:26)

"Our Father, which art in heaven" was how I began the Lord's Prayer. "Father" was used by many who prayed in church. I understood that God was my "heavenly Father", but how could I know what that meant from an earthly perspective?

Whether I realized, reckoned, or understood the relationship that existed didn't matter, he was still my Father. He spoke to me during my middle teenage years through his Word and his Spirit. He told me of purpose and meaning in Christ so that I might know life in all its abundance.

But when I reached the later teenage years, I felt I no longer wanted that relationship. My plans and dreams could be accomplished just fine by my own efforts.

Take a snapshot right here of my condition. Consider that frame as a frame of mind and heart. Compare it, in an earthly sense, to my relationship as a son to my dad. When

I reached 18 to 20 years of age, I suddenly believed myself to be a man, which implied that independence and self-sufficiency would follow. I was no longer under the "control" of my dad. But does that mean that he ceased being my dad? Does that mean that he ceased caring about me, ceased loving me, and ceased wanting the best for me?

What was my heavenly Father's role at this time? Did the relationship dissolve simply because I no longer wanted him as a part of my life? Certainly it did not! Just as my dad was still my dad, my heavenly Father was still my Father. However, my role as obedient son changed into the wandering, rebellious role of prodigal son.

Just as my earthly father stepped aside and allowed my independence, so, also, did my heavenly Father. Over the next two decades I would learn of a Father who refused to undo a relationship that was bound for eternity.

The period I spent as a prodigal was marked with many attempts to find another purpose and meaning in my life. My Father, though, simply would not allow me to find peace and rest in any other condition or relationship. Yet, I kept trying and searching for meaning outside of the Father's will. I thought obedience to a higher authority did not apply to me.

Read the explanation found in Hebrews 12, and the Father's role during this wayward period comes into focus:

You have forgotten that word of encouragement that addresses you as sons: "My son, do not make light of the Lord's discipline, and do not lose heart when he rebukes you, be-

cause the Lord disciplines those he loves, and punishes everyone he accepts as a son." (Hebrews 12:5–6)

Discipline and punishment were applied to my life as a prodigal. Was God being mean and hateful? Read the words again: "The Lord disciplines those he loves." **He loves** me as a Father loves his son, and he simply wouldn't give up on me. His love knows no limits. "And he punishes everyone he accepts as a son." He had accepted me as a SON. I could not change the relationship. As much as I tried, it simply was impossible to change my relationship as his son. So I experienced his punishment administered in boundless love.

Listen further to the words from Hebrews 12:

If you are not disciplined (and everyone undergoes discipline), then you are illegitimate children and not true sons. (Hebrews 12:8)

As a true son, I knew discipline. Although rebellion kept me from knowing the closeness of the relationship during those years, the relation did not change in my prodigal state.

Thankfully, the story does not end in that state. The prodigal son came home. And in that homecoming, I learned the depth of my Father's love and mercy. Nothing could have prepared me for that moment of restoration. I considered myself worthless. I had wasted all the opportunities that God had provided. I had rebelled and walked away from the One who wanted the very best for me. How could he possibly take me back as a member of the family?

BUT HE DID! In that moment I knew the overwhelming freedom of forgiveness and the full restoration of fellowship and closeness with my Father. He welcomed me back, not as slave, but as a SON. Even more, my Father threw a celebration. Later I would re-read the parable of the prodigal son (Luke 15), and realize from a new perspective that there was a celebration upon my return. In the preceding parable of the lost coin, Jesus says these words:

> *"In the same way, I tell you, there is rejoicing in the presence of the angels of God over one sinner who repents." (Luke 15:10)*

What a loving Father I have! He threw a celebration! How can I forget that welcome back? How can I desire any life other than that of an obedient and faithful son? Now I understand the **SPIRIT OF SONSHIP**.

What a loving Father we all have as sons and daughters! Before we came to salvation through the Cross of Christ, we were slaves to sin and could not know a Holy Father. Jesus tells us:

> *"I tell you the truth, everyone who sins is a slave to sin. Now a slave has no permanent place in the family, but a son belongs to it forever. So if the Son sets you free you will be free indeed." (John 8:34–36)*

We have been freed from the slavery of sin; yet, we become more than just freed slaves. God makes us sons and daughters in his family **forever**. And in that relationship we become his heirs:

> *But when the time had fully come, God sent his son, born of a woman, born under law, to redeem those under law, that we might receive the full rights of sons.*
> *Because you are sons, God sent the Spirit of his son into our hearts, the Spirit who calls out, "Abba, Father." So you*

are no longer a slave, but a son; and since you are a son, God has made you also an heir. (Galatians 4:4–7)

Put those verses in you heart! Through faith in Jesus Christ we are made sons and daughters of God (Galatians 3:26). And he placed in our hearts the Spirit of his Son. And that Spirit is the same who addresses God as "Abba, Father". "Abba" is Aramaic for father, but its use parallels our use of the very personal "daddy". Jesus addressed his Father with that personal name:

"Abba, Father," he said, "everything is possible for you. Take this cup from me. Yet not what I will, but what you will." (Mark 14:36)

Because the Spirit of his Son is within us, we, also, may call out and may know the personal "ABBA". He desires and enables a relationship that is close and personal and eternal, and it is found in surrender to his **Fatherly** will.

It is simple. He is our Father. As believers, we are his sons and daughters, forever. His love and mercy and grace for us know no bounds or end. He will never forsake us.

I can testify to this truth.

LET US LIVE, THEREFORE, IN THE SPIRIT OF SONSHIP.

YOUR TURN:

(1) Have you fully recognized (reckoned) this relationship in your own life?
(2) Through the Spirit of sonship, address your heavenly father as Abba.
(3) Please read Romans 8:12–17.
(4) Please read Matthew 5:44–45, and Mark 3:33–34.
(5) If you have wandered from the Father's will, make the move now to return. Is there celebrating in heaven?
(6) Pray that you will know in increasing measure the relationship as one of God's children.

Epilogue

I hope that God has blessed you through this book. It was designed for your response during the reading, and that response should continue. Write the following words of Paul in your heart as you close these pages:

> *I want to know Christ and the power of his resurrection and the fellowship of sharing in his sufferings, becoming like him in his death, and so, somehow, to attain to the resurrection from the dead.*
>
> *Not that I have already obtained all this, or have already been made perfect, but I press on to take hold of that for which Christ Jesus took hold of me. Brothers, I do not consider myself yet to have taken hold of it. But one thing I do; Forgetting what is behind and straining toward what is ahead, I press on toward the goal to win the prize for which God has called me heavenward in Christ Jesus.*
>
> Philippians 3:10–14

It would be an encouragement for me to hear from you. Let me know how I can pray for you in your walk with the Lord.

OUT OF A DISTANT LAND

PRESS ON!

Gary Bond
Sonship Service
408 Peachtree St.
Johnson City, TN 37604
sonshipauctions@hotmail.com

To order additional copies of

OUT OF A DISTANT LAND

Have your credit card ready and call:

1-877-421-READ (7323)

or please visit our web site at
www.pleasantword.com

Also available at: www.amazon.com

Printed in the United States
66954LVS00002B